LLEWELLYN'S

Little Book of

MOON

SPELLS

Andrew Harris

Melanie Marquis is an award-winning author, lifelong practitioner of magick, and local coordinator for the Pagan Pride Project. She's the author of *Carl Llewellyn Weschcke: Pioneer and Publisher of Body, Mind, and Spirit*, *A Witch's World of Magick*, *The Witch's Bag of Tricks*, *Beltane*, and *Lughnasadh*, as well as co-author of *Witchy Mama* (with Emily A. Francis) and creator of the *Modern Spellcaster's Tarot* (illustrated by Scott Murphy), all from Llewellyn Worldwide. In addition to her books, Melanie offers tarot readings, handwriting analysis, witchcraft services, and customized classes in tarot and magick. She is also the creator and producer of the Mystical Minds Convention.

LLEWELLYN'S
Little Book of

MOON
SPELLS

MELANIE MARQUIS

LLEWELLYN PUBLICATIONS
WOODBURY, MINNESOTA

FIRST EDITION
Fourth Printing, 2021

Cover cartouche by Freepik
Cover design by Shira Atakpu
Interior art by Llewellyn Art Department

Llewellyn Publications is a registered trademark of Llewellyn Worldwide Ltd.

Library of Congress Cataloging-in-Publication Data
Names: Marquis, Melanie, author.
Title: Llewellyn's little book of moon spells / Melanie Marquis.
Description: First edition. | Woodbury, Minnesota : Llewellyn Publishing,
2020. | Includes bibliographical references. |
Identifiers: LCCN 2020014991 (print) | LCCN 2020014992 (ebook) | ISBN
9780738762456 (paperback) | ISBN 9780738762616 (ebook)
Subjects: LCSH: Magic. | Moon—Miscellanea.
Classification: LCC BF1623.M66 M35 2020 (print) | LCC BF1623.M66 (ebook)
| DDC 133.4/3—dc23
LC record available at https://lccn.loc.gov/2020014991
LC ebook record available at https://lccn.loc.gov/2020014992

Llewellyn Worldwide Ltd. does not participate in, endorse, or have any authority or responsibility concerning private business transactions between our authors and the public.

All mail addressed to the author is forwarded, but the publisher cannot, unless specifically instructed by the author, give out an address or phone number.

Any internet references contained in this work are current at publication time, but the publisher cannot guarantee that a specific location will continue to be maintained. Please refer to the publisher's website for links to authors' websites and other sources.

Llewellyn Publications
A Division of Llewellyn Worldwide Ltd.
2143 Wooddale Drive
Woodbury, MN 55125-2989
www.llewellyn.com

Printed in China

Contents

(

Spells

Other Magic

Potions

Powders

Acknowledgments

Thank you to everyone at Llewellyn for helping to make this book a success, and for allowing me the pleasure and honor of writing it. Thank you also to Joy Vernon for sharing with me your insights into astrology, and special thanks to my children Aidan and Mia for being so nice to me all the time, no matter what phase the moon is in.

This book is dedicated to everyone who feels the call of the moon.

INTRODUCTION
The Magical Moon

Have you ever felt inspired or excited by a bright full moon, or found comfort and hope in the silvery glow of a crescent moon shining through a thin veil of clouds? As our closest celestial neighbor and the brightest, biggest object in the night sky, the moon has an undeniable connection to the planet we all call home. In fact, life as we know it literally depends on it.

Not only does the moon move the oceans and produce the tides through its gravitational pull, but it also actually lengthens the day by tempering the speed at which our planet spins on its axis. It can be easy in modern times to take the moon for granted, but we need it just as much as we always have, even though some of our needs have evolved.

Before humankind learned to harness the power of electricity, full moon nights held the significance of enabling activity much later than was otherwise possible, long after the fire had died down. The bright light of a full moon invites adventure, secret meetings, arts and crafts, storytelling—all the things that are hard to fit into a day-time filled with work and a nighttime consumed in dark-ness. Although we no longer rely on the moon as the sole way to light up the night, the moon still seems to awaken something primal and magical within us, inviting us to plunge into the unknown to discover something mysteri-ous and unexpected. In today's world of hustle and bus-tle, the moon gives us a much-needed reminder to look up, just as it inspires us to look within.

Carl Llewellyn Weschcke, New Age visionary, author, and former owner and CEO of Llewellyn Worldwide, described the movement of the moon and planets as being "Nature's own clock." In a very practical and physi-cal sense, what we see in the sky above gives us guidance as to what we will find below. Our observation of the moon's cycle gives a rhythm and pattern to life, providing us with a visible way to mark the changing of seasons and the passing of days. Attuning to the rhythm of the moon allows us to make the most of the opportunities that each moment in time provides, enabling us to plan the best route forward to our desired destination.

In this book, you'll find many ways to use the power of the moon to actively enrich your own life experiences while enriching and transforming the world as a whole. Instead of feeling stuck when you stumble against one of fate's many roadblocks, you'll learn to attune to the influencing and influenceable tides of destiny and transform troublesome situations into opportunities that work in your favor. This is the art of magic.

Despite pop culture implications, magic isn't actually scary, spooky, or impossible. In fact, anyone can do it and it won't require years of difficult training or expensive or complex tools. Magic is simply the act of using your own personal power and the power of the universe to transform and guide the energies that make up all that is. Moon magic is any type of magic that uses the moon's power to help you do just that.

Analogous to the subconscious mind and psychic awareness, the moon epitomizes the abilities we rely on most heavily in a magical working (also called a spell). Even to people completely new to the art of magic, the moon can be a ready springboard that quickly launches you out of the mundane and into the mystical.

To witches who work magic with the powers of nature, the moon has always held a special significance. Many people of the past and present share a view of the moon as a manifestation of divinity, and some of the earliest known deities are goddesses and gods of the moon. As the roughly 28-day menstrual cycle somewhat mirrors the ebb and flow of the moon, it's only natural that the moon be equated with human sexuality and our own fertility and survival as a species.

The moon has also been conceived as the home of the dead, the dwelling place of our ancestors and a place of temporary respite for souls awaiting the next cycle of rebirth into life on earth. Whatever the moon might mean to you personally, and whether or not you have ever considered that the moon may have a power even stronger than its gravity, you can learn how to deepen and strengthen your connection to the moon to produce immediate benefits in your everyday life.

In this book, you'll find a plethora of ways to work with the power of the magical moon. Beginning with an overview of moon magic basics and some ideas for strengthening your lunar connections, you'll also find information on correspondences and how to time your magic with the moon. Spells are arranged so that they're easy to find when you need them, with a section of spells organized by moon phase, and a section of spells organized by magical goal. You'll also find a chapter on lunar potions and powders, as well as a chapter on magic especially designed for lunar eclipses, supermoons, and other special occurrences. In the last chapter, you'll find a guide to moon magic throughout the year, with ideas for making the most of the seasonal flow, lunar symbols, and a full moon and new moon spell for each month.

Moon magic is a spiritual practice that can be very rewarding. As you practice the spells in this book, believe in your abilities and set your goals as high as the moon!

THE RABBIT IN THE MOON

Many cultures have stories about a rabbit in the moon. In Chinese folklore, the Jade Rabbit is said to be the faithful companion of the moon goddess, Chang'O. The two dwell on the moon together, where the Jade Rabbit mixes immortality potions. There is an earlier Buddhist legend that tells the story of the Buddha's incarnation as a white rabbit. This rabbit was so good and generous that he offered up his own body as food for the gods. Moved by the rabbit's willingness to sacrifice his own life, the god Shakra didn't eat the rabbit, but instead honored him by carving his image into the face of the moon as a reminder of the pious act of sacrifice.

There is a similar legend in Mexican folklore involving the Aztec god Quetzalcóatl. The god had transformed into a human so that he could visit the earth. After walking for a great distance, Quetzalcóatl was tired and hungry, so he sat down to rest. A small rabbit spotted the weary man, and hopped over to check on him. The rabbit noticed the man's hunger, and offered himself as food. Quetzalcóatl declined the offer to eat the rabbit, but he lifted him up so high in honor that his image was forever after imprinted upon the face of the moon.

Chapter One

MOON MAGIC BASICS

In order to make moon magic, you need to be able to connect to the energies of the moon and entice those energies to cooperate with you. If you're not able to sense the moon's energies, it will be very difficult to use those energies in a magical way! If, on the other hand, you forge a connection to the moon that allows you to actually feel those lunar energies in your heart and soul, your moon-powered spells will literally work like a charm, producing swift results. In this chapter, you'll find some ways to explore and expand your lunar connections, as well as some basics for making magic with the moon.

Discovering Lunar Connections

We are all unique beings, and we each connect with lunar energies in our own unique ways. Exploring your affinities, gifts, and preferences when it comes to moon magic will help you broaden your options and develop your strengths. Answer these questions to discover a little more about yourself and your natural connections to the moon:

1. Do you have a favorite phase of the moon, such as full moon or waxing crescent moon?

2. Do you ever notice that your moods and thought patterns seem to shift with the changing moon phases? For example, some people tend to feel more introspective and withdrawn during the waning phase, and more energetic and excitable during the waxing moon and full moon phase.

3. What words might you use to describe the moon and the feeling it gives you when you gaze at it or contemplate it?

4. Different colors have been associated with the moon for use in moon magic. Using your own

intuition and knowledge of the moon, what color or colors do you think best serve to symbolize the moon? What feelings and associations do you have with these colors?

5. Different animals have been associated with the moon, including rabbits, owls, cats, and wolves. Does the moon bring to mind any animal associations for you?

6. Have you ever seen a landscape or found a stone or smelled a scent that reminds you of the moon?

7. Imagine that you are outside at night having the most wonderful time you can possibly envision. In your mind's eye, look up at the sky. What does the moon look like in your fantasy of the best time ever?

8. Moon magic can utilize many different mediums, including potions, powders, crystal magic, symbols and sigils, spoken charms, musical magic, and more. Do you have any favorite mediums for moon magic? Are there different mediums you would like to try?

9. What benefits do you think it might bring to attune your magical workings to harmonize with the moon's natural ebb and flow?

Strengthening Lunar Connections

One of the most effective and obvious ways to strengthen your connections to the moon is to spend as much time as possible outside in the moonlight, simply observing the moon and being present in the moment. Work to broaden your perspective and establish new associations and understandings of the moon. You might study moon lore from different cultures around the world, watch documentaries about the moon, or read moon-themed poems. You can also build upon the connections to the moon that you have already established. If, for instance, the sight of a full moon makes you imagine the music of a pan flute, you might try playing one in the moonlight as a preliminary to your spellcasting. If the moon brings to mind images of a sly fox sneaking noiselessly through a forest or an owl gliding majestically through the night sky, you might consider incorporating these animal symbols into your moon magic. Another way to deepen and expand your lunar connections is to learn

Dye your hair on the the first Friday following the new moon for longest-lasting results.

more about the factual reality of the moon from a scientific and astronomical perspective. We modern seekers are blessed with a trove of readily available resources that enable us to gain great insight into the workings of our solar system. You can find online simulators showing how lunar phases change throughout the moon's monthly orbit, view 3D maps of the moon, track the moon's movement through the heavens in real time, find the local times of moonrise, moonset, full moons, new moons, and much more. Make an effort to learn as much as you can about the moon, and you'll find your ability to utilize lunar energies in your magic quickly increase.

Moon Journal

One very hands-on way to learn more about the moon and your relationship to it is to simply observe the moon frequently, and keep track of your observations. You might dedicate a special notebook or sketchbook to serve as your moon journal. Each day for a month or more, make a sketch of the moon showing its phase and relative position to your vantage point, noting the date and time. When you do so, think about where the sun is located in relation to the earth and moon. This will give you a better understanding of lunar phases and why the moon appears to us as it does. You might also note in your moon journal any significant events or unusual occurrences for each day, perhaps describing your general mood and the overall flow of the day. After you do this for a while, you will have a valuable chronicle of personal experiences and corresponding lunar phases to analyze for any significant patterns or unexpected connections that may inform both your magical practice and your everyday dealings.

Magical Basics

While there's great truth in the statement that there's no right or wrong way to do magic, it can be argued that there is in fact a "right way" and a "wrong way": If your magic works, you know you're doing it the "right way," but if it falls flat or does something entirely contrary to what you intended, you know that something certainly did go wrong along the way! The variety of forms and possibilities for these right and wrong ways, however, is truly infinite. Even the most skilled and experienced magical practitioners have failures sometimes, and it can be difficult to pinpoint the exact cause of a spell not working as expected, just as it is equally difficult to explain exactly how or why a particular spell succeeded. A way to bring growth in your magical practice is to let both your failures *and* your successes inform you and inspire you. Note what doesn't work, and try something different the next time. If a certain method works for you, use it freely without any need for validation from spellbooks or other practitioners. We are all different— what works for some might not work so well for others. Honor your own magic and get to know your own "right ways" of doing spellwork.

While the written instructions for a particular spell can give you ideas and inspiration for the outward form of the magic, it's difficult bordering on impossible to describe in words the internal process that must take place in the heart and mind of the practitioner in order for magic to be made. Without the internal process, the outward method may accomplish very little or nothing. This isn't always the case, as certain things do have inherent magical power and certain magic does happen automatically. Most commonly, however, it's the practitioner's heart and mind that are the key ingredients in any magical working—not the tools, nor the words, nor the particulars of the method.

This internal action that magic requires might be described as imprinting one's will upon selected energies, programming those energies to act as directed. The universe is composed of different vibrations, groupings, patterns, and waves of energy that are inherently transformable and directable. Physics defines *energy* in simplest terms as "the ability to do work," while *work* can be defined as "the ability to transfer or transform one form of energy into another form of energy." Energy itself is thus the potential to transform and apply itself to different forms and purposes, while magic can be considered a way to influence energy into taking on whatever form and purpose chosen for it.

The heart of many spellcastings boils down to a single moment: when you are simultaneously thinking clearly of your intention, feeling the emotions that accompany that intention, amplifying the energy of those thoughts and emotions as much as possible—and then sending that energy into the astral plane from which the manifest world emerges, which will in turn respond by creating these new energy patterns as per your instructions here in the manifest world. The many other aspects of magic, such as the candles, herbs, potions, rituals, and verses, are all intended to support the achievement of that one most critical magical moment, adding power to your working, honing your mind, and heightening your emotions so that there will be enough fuel and clarity to ensure a successful spellcasting.

In the case of moon magic, much of the spell's so-called fuel comes from the energy of the moon itself, and often words, stones, symbols, plants and other items are used to help forge and strengthen the spell's connection to this natural and tremendous source of power. A great deal of spellwork is based upon principles of sympathetic or imitative magic. Through ritual and spellcraft, we mimic as best we can the essence of the realities and potentialities we would like to create, the idea being that in doing so, we make an impression on the astral levels that will in turn create a vibration or forge a connection conducive to bringing forth what it is we desire here in the physical world.

The astral might be seen as not so much the great beyond, but rather, the great within. When we work magic, we are conscious of a deeper level of reality, a power and pattern that resides within us and within all things. The universe we're experiencing may be but the reflection upon the surface of a river that runs much deeper than we can fathom, the planets and stars the uppermost leaves upon the highest branches of the Tree of Life that grows upon the river's banks. Through magic, we strengthen and expand the roots between our world and the astral plane from which our everyday reality grows.

Such rituals also have effects that may be more mundane than magical but certainly help do the trick in getting you what you want, nonetheless. By performing a spell or ritual, we are using and connecting our subconscious and conscious minds, which in turn has the effect of helping us to truly believe in ourselves and act with confidence—not to mention making us more likely to actually take the actions that can make possible the success we're hoping to achieve. It's important to understand that magic doesn't give us an automatic pass from everyday duties and actions. It's essential both before and after doing a spellcasting to take mundane measures to achieve your goals, as well. Pinpoint the steps you can take to get you closer to your aim, then take those steps one by one as your magic does its bit behind the scenes to exponentially magnify and multiply the positive results of your efforts. Even if it's a tiny baby step like "do further research," identifying any actions you can take right away and then taking those actions without delay is going to quickly get you moving ever closer to your goal. If your physical actions don't show commitment to your magical actions, your magic is likely to fall short of expectations.

WAXING OR WANING?

You can quickly tell if the moon is waxing or waning by noticing the direction in which the "horns" of the crescent point. If the tips of the crescent point towards the left, the moon is waxing, whereas if they point to the right, the moon is waning. You can use this rhyme to help you remember:

Horns to the east, moonlight decrease.

Horns to the west, the moon grows best.

A moon spell can be as simple as a quick and spontaneous prayer to the moon coupled with an emotionally-charged visualization, or it might involve repeating a series of complex steps in the course of a month-long ritual. Don't look at spell instructions as strict guidelines, but rather use them as suggestions to the form your moon magic might take. When you encounter a new spell, try to evaluate each step and each component to determine its role and function in the magical process. Once you're able to do that, you'll be able to find effective substitutions for any portions of a spell you would like to adapt or improve, which will give you a lot more room for customization and flexibility in your moon magic.

Preparing for Moon Magic

While moon magic doesn't necessarily require any advanced preparation, they do require you to be able to get into what might be described as a *magical mindset*— a state of being in which you feel confident in your ability to effect change in the Universe through the cooperative power of your spirit and those powers of nature with which you choose to work. Some practitioners can get into this mindset instantaneously without any difficulty or preparation, while others might need or simply want to spend more time on this stage of the process so that they feel more ready for the magic at hand. One part of getting into a magical mindset is to step away from your regular, everyday thought patterns. If you have a lot of things on your mind, it can be helpful to jot down a list of your worries along with any solutions or action steps you might take regarding them. Or you might simply place your hands on the ground and think of your worries and any other negative feelings exiting your body, flowing into the neutralizing and healing ground. The other half of getting into a magical mindset involves actually getting into a higher level of consciousness. You might accomplish this automatically if your mind is trained to do so, or you might accomplish this through meditation, listening to mystical music, creating a magical atmosphere, putting on special clothing, drumming, dancing, sitting outside for a while, or taking a moonlit stroll. Try different things and see what works best for you. Many practitioners find benefit in taking a pre-ritual magical bath attuned to the energies of the spellcasting to come. You might try a simple moon bath to help you get into a magical mindset before a lunar working.

Moon Bath

This is an energizing and cleansing bath that will leave you feeling purified and empowered. Enjoy it before a lunar ritual or whenever you need to relax and shift out of a dull and dragging mood. Fill the tub with warm water and add a squeeze of juice from a fresh lemon as well as a few drops of vanilla extract or a spoonful of vanilla powder. As you bathe, think of the moonlight and how you feel under a starry moonlit sky. Invite these energies to enter into your body. When the bath is complete, put on special clothing or jewelry that you associate with magic or the moon. Silver, gray, black, purple, or white are popular color choices for moon magic. You may want to add silver jewelry or symbols of the moon to your attire.

• • •

Creating a Special Place for Moon Magic

Intuitively and ideally, outdoors under a moonlit sky is the obvious and usually preferable location for lunar-themed magical workings. This isn't always possible or practical, however. The weather could be terrible, and you might find it difficult to get into a magical mindset while you're shivering cold or being drenched with rain! You might not have a safe outdoor space available in which to do magic in an obvious way. It might be that the moon won't be visible on a given night or that it will be visible at a time when you're not able to go outdoors. There are many reasons why you might decide that an indoor lunar working is called for, which is a perfectly acceptable alternative that has its own advantages. Doing magic indoors allows you to more easily keep spell items in place for a period of time without those items being disturbed. As moon spells are often tied to the cycles of the moon, some workings require multiple steps to be completed over multiple days as the moon waxes or wanes, or a magical talisman you're creating might need to charge for the entirety of a monthly moon cycle. If you have an indoor area dedicated to your magic, you can leave out whatever spell components you like for as long as you like, without having to worry about wind, squirrels, or too many random curious people inadvertently interfering with your magical working.

To bring good luck, spin the rings on your fingers when you first see the sliver of the new moon.

Whether outdoors or indoors, frequently doing magic in the same place imparts to that place a magical power of its own that will contribute to the overall effectiveness of your spellwork. If you don't yet have your own special space dedicated to magic, don't despair—you can get many of the same benefits by using the same ritual tools repeatedly, even if you end up using those tools in different areas. You can also choose to keep all your ritual tools and altar implements in a single box, so that the box itself becomes a mobile altar of sorts. You can even leave spell components in place within a dresser drawer, creating a hidden magical space that you can slide in and out of existence or just as easily store your socks in.

Whether it's a mobile altar or a dedicated indoor or outdoor ritual space, you'll want to do something or several things to make that space into a space for magic. Even laying out your ritual tools in a mindful way will help create the atmosphere you desire. Consider placing items in your moon magic space that resonate with lunar symbolism that makes sense to you. Ask yourself: What stones remind you of the moon? What colors, what scents, what animals, what numbers, what deities or spirits or archetypes do you personally associate with the moon? Here are some items you might consider including in a lunar altar space or a mobile moon magic toolkit:

ALTAR CLOTH: A cloth of any size you like that can be spread out to create an area in which to work magic and place your spell implements and ingredients. For moon magic, you might consider a cloth of silver, or something with a shiny or iridescent quality. For waning moon magic or dark moon magic, you might go with a black cloth. For waxing moon magic or new moon magic, a white cloth would be a good fit. For full moon magic, you might choose to use a red or gold cloth. Using a circular cloth that mirrors the shape of the moon rather than a square or rectangular cloth will also add more symbolism and power to your lunar workings.

STONES, CRYSTALS, AND HERBS: Stones, crystals, and plants of all types each have their own energetic signatures and effects that can add power to magical rituals with little effort on the part of the spellcaster. While stones and herbs are even more effective when empowered with your emotionally-charged intentions, they have inherent power that will help fuel your magic simply by their presence. Arrange them around a ritual space to help create a magical atmosphere and raise the overall vibration, or incorporate them into spells for their unique effects or to reflect and express the intentions of your magic. Stones and plants to be used in moon magic can be empowered by placing them outside in the moonlight. Think of the purpose the stone or plant will serve in your magical working, and envision that essence within the plant or stone magnifying, amplified and fine-tuned by the moon's own powerful vibration.

CANDLES: One of the quickest ways to create a magical atmosphere is to simply light a candle. The act of burning a candle with intention and focus can be a spellcasting in and of itself, making them indispensable to troves of magical practitioners everywhere. Candles can be carved, anointed with potions or oils, or selected for their color symbolism or shape. They might be burned to symbolize a diminishing and banishing effect, or they might be burned to symbolize energy being raised and magnified. The versatility of candles is a huge part of their popularity. In a lunar working, you might utilize candles to symbolize the light reflected off the moon, or to represent the magical power that the moon holds within her. Consider a selection of candles in gray, white, silver, and black. Spherical candles that mimic the shape of the moon can also be useful.

STATUARY: Many practitioners enjoy decorating their magical spaces with statuary depicting real or mythical animals, gods, goddesses, and other archetypes. Doing so can help provide a focal point for spellwork and rituals that also helps to strengthen one's connections to the particular entity, animal, or archetype depicted. For a lunar altar, you might consider statues of a moon goddess such as Hecate or Isis, or a figurine of an animal associated with the moon such as a rabbit or bat. Your statuary need not be particularly reverent to do its work. If you're a fan of the manga character Sailor Moon, for instance, you might choose to include a Sailor Moon figurine amongst your altar items to remind you that you, too, have the power to fight evil by moonlight!

RITUAL TOOLS: Ritual tools include a wide array of items that may be utilized in the course of your magical practice. Common tools of modern witches include a wand (associated with the air element), a blade (associated with the fire element), a pentacle (associated with the earth element), and a cup or cauldron (associated with the water element). In moon magic, the cup or cauldron are especially useful, as these water-associated items are also associated with the moon and its goddesses.

Casting a Circle

Whether you choose to go all out in decorating your ritual space, or whether you prefer to simply find a big tree to hide behind and do your spellwork on the fly, it's very beneficial to prepare the area for the magical working. One way to do so is through the act of casting a circle. A circle in this sense is a spherical area of high vibrational energy that extends both above and below the ground, forming a protected, safe, and sacred space in which to work magic. The benefit of preparing the magical space through casting a circle is that not only does it help to keep unwanted energies out, it also helps to keep desired energies in. Just as it would be difficult to make soup without a pot, even if you had all the right ingredients, the same logic applies here. Casting a circle creates an invisibly enclosed area that contains and concentrates the power of the magic as the practitioner works the spell at hand.

Casting a circle involves removing from the area unwanted energies and inviting into the space whatever energies and powers you do wish to welcome there. You can accomplish this process through the application of psychic awareness, will, and personal power. Stand in the center of the area in which you wish to cast the circle. Open yourself to the feeling of the space as it is currently. Do you sense any negative energies? Can the energy of the space be improved? Use your mind, heart, and magical senses to guide you as you move slowly around the circle, extending your arm in front of you and projecting through your palm a radiant, love-filled energy. Envision this energy filling the spherical space around you, above you, and below you, driving out any negative vibrations. Imagine this space as a sealed, contained, and protected area in which nothing unwanted can enter.

Next, focus on the powers or energies that you wish to invite into this sacred space. You might feel drawn to calling on elemental forces, planetary energies, deities, or ancestral spirits. You can use your own words of invitation or utilize a more formal invocation. You might place items such as stones, statues, photographs, or candles around the space to symbolize each power or energy that you wish to invite. There are much fancier ways to cast a circle, but this is generally the gist of it.

Other simple methods of circle casting include setting out a circle of stones, crystals, or candles, envisioning this as a ring of power that keeps out any unwelcome energies, or placing a symbol of one of the four elements at each of the cardinal directions: incense for air in the east, a candle for fire in the south, a cup or cauldron for water in the west, and a stone or pentacle for earth in the north.

Drawing Down the Moon

"Drawing down the moon" is a phrase used in witchcraft practice to describe the act of calling into one's self the power and spirit of the great goddess who claims the moon in all its phases as one of her many manifestations. This goddess may be conceived as an independently existing deity or understood in a more abstract and conceptual way as an encapsulation of various energies, essences, qualities, ideas, or functions and aspects of nature. Drawing down the moon requires you to attune your energies to harmonize with the power that is to be invoked, and to make space within yourself for those powers to enter and operate. You might simply stand under the moon with your arms lifted skyward, letting the essence of the moonlight fill your being as you strive to match your own vibrations to this manifestation of nature's amazing power. Invite the power that is encapsulated and reflected by the moon to pour into your body. Honoring your own comfort level and peace of mind, make as much room within yourself for this energy to reign as you are willing and able to do. If you prefer a more formal or traditional method, you can find many beautiful and elaborate "drawing down the moon" rituals in witchcraft books and online sources. There are several benefits and purposes of drawing down the moon. The practitioner may receive or channel direct messages from the divine and astral planes, magical power is strengthened, and psychic awareness is sent into hyper-mode—all of which can be of great benefit in your lunar-themed spellcastings.

Chapter Two

LUNAR
CORRESPONDENCES

Correspondences are an important and effective way to weave the connecting threads that make magic possible. For example, say you want to use the moon's magic to help attract love to your life. You can't literally bring down the moon and place it on your altar, but you can use a stone that has lunar qualities to act as a sort of stand-in for the moon. The part of "love" might be played by a selection of rose petals that you then move toward yourself with the lunar stone as a way to symbolize the moon attracting to you what you wish. By mimicking in the physical realm the designs we wish to weave within the astral, we create a thread of connection that opens a corridor through which the reality we desire may manifest. Correspondences may be based on physical appearance, physical qualities, elemental affinities, proximity, or magical attributes. For example, a round and porous gray stone may be chosen for a lunar spell due to its resemblance to the moon's cratered surface. Likewise, the reflective surface of a mirror makes it a fitting lunar symbol as it calls to mind how the moon reflects the sunlight. A piece of aquamarine, associated with the element of water, might be used to forge a connection with the moon, which is said to have rulership over that element. A bird might be chosen as a lunar symbol because it spends so much time in the sky moving through the heavens with ease, just like the moon. As it resonates with a loving, dreamy vibration, a jasmine flower harmonizes perfectly with certain attributes of the lunar essence. Magical correspondences may even be based on entirely personal reasons you're unlikely to find in a spellbook.

While traditional correspondences are traditional for a reason (they've been found to be effective after centuries of practical trial and error), there is still no substitute for your own personal system of symbols. The glyphs, symbols, and correspondences that resonate with us are influenced by numerous factors including culture, personal experience, and personality; symbolism that makes sense to you on an intellectual and emotional level will be the most successful in your magic. If something helps you to feel connected with the energies of the moon or reflects the intention of your magical working, then it will be an appropriate and effective symbol to use in your moon magic. Look to traditional or otherwise recommended correspondences as a general guide and starting point for finding ideas worthy of further exploration and consideration, but let your gut feelings be the ultimate decision-maker when it comes to choosing correspondences for your spells.

The correspondences described in this chapter are intended to inspire your magic rather than restrict it. Note that the correspondences of the items listed here are not limited solely to lunar associations; they have many other attributes and associations. Many plants, stones, and animals, for instance, have associations with both the sun and the moon or with multiple elements. While most of the correspondences offered here are based on established moon lore and magical tradition, they are also influenced

MOON DREAMS

To dream of a bright waxing moon can prophecy love and success.

Dreaming of a full moon can be seen as a sign of happy times ahead.

To dream of a red moon may be a premonition of coming wealth or renown.

Dreaming of a moon obscured by clouds can signal trouble ahead, or it can be seen as a message that something is being hidden from your view.

by the author's own personal experiences and instincts in witchcraft. To make an exhaustive list of correspondences that everyone can agree on is an impossible feat, as our personal systems of symbology are as numerous and different as we are! Take the lunar correspondences in this chapter as suggestions, and let your own intuition and experience be the ultimate judge.

Natural Places

Queen of the night and ruler of the elements of water and earth, the moon has long been associated with dark places and areas where natural water sources can be found. The moon might also be associated with hilltops, circular clearings, and graveyards.

- Oceans
- Seas
- Rivers
- Lakes
- Ponds
- Streams
- Springs
- Wells
- Barrows
- Valleys
- Canyons
- Caves
- Hilltops
- Circular clearings
- Fairy rings (naturally occurring circular growths of mushrooms)

Animals

Animals associated with the moon include nocturnal animals due to their connection with the night, animals and insects that enjoy digging or live underground or in caves due to their association with darkness and the underworld, flying birds and insects due to their proximity to the heavens, creatures of the water such as waterfowl and fish due to their elemental association with the moon's corresponding element, and animals that appear to easily adapt, transform, or shapeshift by way of being amphibious or undergoing a metamorphosis or having the ability to regenerate, as these qualities are reminiscent of the moon's swift, smooth, and constant change of phase.

- Crab
- Frog
- Fish
- Oyster
- Clam
- Turtle
- Chameleon
- Snake
- Otter

- Duck
- Heron
- Owl
- Bat
- Bee
- Beetle
- Moth
- Panther
- Coyote

- Wolf
- Bull
- Cow
- Cat
- Rabbit
- Dog

- Goat
- Racoon
- Fox
- Rat
- Weasel
- Beaver

Otherworldly and Mythical Beings

Otherworldly and mythical beings associated with water, air, the night, or immortality are often considered to be lunar in nature.

- Mermaids
- Dragons
- Fairies
- Unicorns

- Ghosts
- Werewolves
- Banshees

Trees

Trees deemed to be lunar are usually those trees that grow in or near water due to their elemental associations, trees with white bark due to their being the color of the moon, fruit-producing trees due to their association with sexuality and fertility, and trees with waxy leaves due to their reflective qualities in moonlight.

- Willow
- Elm
- Yew
- Palm
- Holly
- Elder

- Hawthorn
- Apple
- Cherry
- Juniper
- Magnolia
- Eucalyptus

Plants

Other lunar-associated plants include night-blooming flowers, plants that grow beneath the ground (such as potatoes), plants that lie low to the earth, plants with crescent-shaped leaves, plants with white flowers, plants with a high water content, and plants with sweet, exotic, or dreamy scents.

- Coconut
- Lemon
- Mushrooms
- Olives
- Cucumbers
- Grapes
- Peas
- Pear

- Peach
- Watercress
- Apple
- Lettuce
- Water chestnuts
- Papaya
- Potato
- Cherry

- Pomegranate
- Apricot
- Plum
- Turnips
- Cabbage
- Jasmine
- Poppy
- Moonflower
- Moonwort
- Mugwort
- Wormwood
- Cannabis

- Mouse-ear chickweed
- Iris
- Violet
- Lily
- Lotus
- Camellia
- Gardenia
- Mesquite
- Mint
- Rose
- Vanilla

Stones

Stones associated with the moon might be chosen for their color, shape, elemental associations, or magical attributes. Shiny, clear, or iridescent stones, round stones, stones that are white, green, blue, gray, or black, stones that are cratered, crescent moon-shaped stones, volcanic stones, triangular stones (due to associations with the feminine/goddess energies), and stones that are found near or in water—as well as those stones that are believed to have attributes associated with that element—can all be considered to have a lunar influence.

- Moonstone
- Selenite
- Serpentine
- Opal
- Quartz crystal
- Jade
- Pearl
- Mother-of-pearl
- Marcasite (white iron pyrite)
- Aquamarine
- Emerald
- Feldspar
- Anorthosite
- Basalt
- Gypsum
- Howlite
- Volcanic stones
- Obsidian

Metals

Silvery metals reminiscent of the color or coolness of moonlight can be deemed to have lunar qualities. Metals such as titanium, aluminum, and iron might be chosen as these oxides are plentiful on the lunar surface.

- Silver
- Aluminum
- Titanium
- Iron

Colors

Many colors can be used to represent the moon. Some color choices are obvious, as the moonlight shines in shades that might be described as white, bluish-white or silver. A full harvest moon on an autumn night might appear a golden saffron yellow. The surface of the moon being gray means that you can find in any shade of gray a suitable correspondence for a lunar working. Other colors associated with the moon that have a less obvious correspondence include red, due to it being the color of the moon during a lunar eclipse, and also being the color of blood (which is said to be ruled by the moon). The color red as a lunar symbol also holds special significance within Wicca. The Triple Goddess of Wicca is seen as having three aspects which equate to the waxing or new moon—symbolized by the Maiden and the color white, the full moon—symbolized by the Mother and the color red, and the waning or dark moon—symbolized

If you break a mirror, bad luck can be averted if you bury the broken pieces at nighttime during a full moon.

by the Crone and the color black. Other color correspondences are based on the magical attributes of the colors being similar to attributes considered to be lunar in quality, such as green for energies of fertility and growth, purple for psychic energies, and blue for wisdom. Blue might also be linked to the moon for reasons of elemental symbolism, blue being the color of water, the element most associated with the moon.

- Red
- White
- Black
- Silver
- Gray

- Saffron yellow
- Blue
- Green
- Purple

Scents

Scents believed to open the psychic faculties and those that have a loving vibration or a sweet, dreamy, or exotic odor can all bring benefits to a lunar working.

- Jasmine
- Vanilla

- Coconut
- Rose

Other Lunar Symbols

People throughout the ages have found lunar symbolism in a vast variety of objects both natural and human-made. Look around your world with fresh eyes and see what reminds you personally of the moon. Lunar symbols might be chosen for qualities of shininess, reflectiveness, or transparency, for an association with water, for having a shape that resembles the moon in any of its phases, for having an association with a lunar deity, or other reasons.

- Shells
- Horns
- Claws
- Coins
- Horseshoe
- Cauldron
- Cup
- Eggs

- Cornucopia
- Crescent shape
- Half-circle shape
- Circle
- Mirror
- Glass
- Scythe
- Round windows

Chapter Three

TIMING MAGIC
WITH THE MOON

The concept of timing is something we all experience and instinctively understand. There is a right
time for some things and a wrong time for some things.
Would you plant flower seeds in the middle of winter
or go roller skating in a lightning storm? It's often obvious when the time is not right for a certain endeavor or
undertaking, but discerning when the time *is* right can be
more of a challenge. Gaining an understanding of lunar
timing will empower you to take the best advantage of

the magical opportunities afforded by the moment—by *any* moment.

Whatever phase the moon is in, wherever in the sky it happens to be, and whether or not you can actually see it at the moment, you can always draw energy and power from the moon to use in your magic. It's not necessary to time your magic based on lunar phases and movements, but it can certainly be helpful and beneficial to do so. Timing your magic with the moon in mind adds another layer of power to your spellwork, using the natural flow of vibrations to give your magic a path of least resistance on which to travel. Just like placing a certain crystal or candle on your altar can help energize a spell, so too can lunar timing offer an additional means of empowering your magic. In this chapter, you'll find some different aspects of lunar timing that you can use to inform and guide your spellcrafting so that your magical workings will have the best chance for success.

Lunar Phases

Probably the most obvious form of lunar timing, and the one we're most likely to be well-acquainted with, is based on the changing phases of the moon. When the moon is full, we feel excitement in the air, a sense of mystery, and an invigorating energy that calls us to reach out for adventure and make some magic. When the moon wanes and diminishes out of view, we may feel introspective, drawn inward, called to meditative and contemplative acts that can lead us to a transformation. The simplest division of lunar phases is to view it as two halves of a whole cycle: the waxing half as the moon approaches its full moon state, and the waning half as the moon approaches its new moon state. These two halves of the lunar cycle can be further divided and described in different ways, and with slightly varying terminology. Here are some common terms used to identify the phases of the moon, and ideas for how you might employ these lunar phases to give your magic an extra boost:

WAXING: The moon is said to be waxing when it is growing larger from the new moon to the full moon. This time period is considered to be ideal for magic intended to increase, manifest, grow, and attract things.

WANING: The moon is said to be waning when it appears to be diminishing from full to new. This time period is great for magic intended to diminish, reduce, remove, restrict, repel, banish, and purify.

DARK MOON AND NEW MOON: While technically a dark and new moon are one and the same—that is, the time when the moon is between the earth and the sun, and thus not illuminated from our viewpoint—in magic, the two terms warrant their own distinctions. The dark moon days, when the moon is entirely invisible to us, have a very different feel from the new moon days, when we see the slimmest sliver of the waxing crescent moon reappear following those days of darkness.

 DARK MOON: The time of the dark moon is a sacred time for many witches. These nights bring us face to face with empty space, the void, and the unknown. We get a feeling that we are cloaked in utter darkness and nothingness—and it is in this nothingness that we may discover our *something-ness*. The dark moon invites us to look inward and process through our darkest shadows. It's also a good opportunity for communicating with spirits of the dead, as well as an ideal time for magical workings intended to banish or bind, especially when defending yourself against powerful negative forces. (In magic, to banish means to push away unwanted energies out of your immediate vicinity so that those energies will no longer be close enough to affect you, whereas to bind means to contain, confine, or restrict unwanted energies in a way that limits the potential effects of these energies to only those specified through your intentions.)

 NEW MOON: Seeing that first sliver of the waxing crescent reappear gives us a new hope, a new energy and a new beginning. This is a great time for magic intended to support the start of new projects, to put things in motion, to attract things to you, to begin to grow things (e.g., love or wealth), to forge new connections, and to deepen existing connections.

 WAXING CRESCENT: This is the name given to the moon when it is somewhere between new moon and the first quarter or half moon. It resembles the shape of a cup, ready to scoop up a refreshing drink to quench your thirst. This lunar phase is great for magic to attain resources and attract to you what you seek. It's also a great opportunity for love magic and spellwork to boost success.

FIRST QUARTER/WAXING HALF-MOON: The term first quarter moon may be a little confusing, as we may naturally assume that the "quarter" refers to one-fourth of the moon's face being illuminated, when in fact it means that half of the moon's face is illuminated. The first quarter moon is the name given to the half-moon in its waxing state between the new moon and the full moon. Waxing half-moons offer a good opportunity to restore equilibrium or to shift the balance of things into your favor. It's also a good chance to evaluate the progress of current projects and endeavors and give them an extra push in the right direction.

WAXING GIBBOUS: This term describes the phase of the moon when it is more than halfway illuminated but not yet full. It resembles a round belly, growing fuller by the day. This stage of the lunar cycle is well-suited to magic to bring prosperity and increase abundance and joy in all aspects of life.

FULL MOON: When the moon's orbital path brings it around to where the sun and moon stand in opposition, with the earth roughly in between, we see the entire face of the moon that is facing earth illuminated, reflecting back to us the rays of the sun. You might think of the full moon as the "whole moon" or "full circle moon." It's a time of culmination and climax, a time of manifestation and magnified magical power. The energy flow seems amped up a notch, thus affording us a wonderful opportunity to try out some of our more ambitious magical workings. The full moon is a good time for magic of all types, as its energies will automatically amplify the power of your spellcasting. Magic that is ambitious; magic to bring things into manifestation; magic to make wishes come true; love and romance magic; and magic to bring success, confidence, power, or protection are especially compatible undertakings for full moon spellcasting.

DISSEMINATING MOON/WANING GIBBOUS: The disseminating moon describes the moon when it is in-between its full and waning half-moon state following the full moon. Also called the waning gibbous phase, the moon is less than full but is still more than halfway illuminated. This is a good time to begin multi-night spells intended to bring a reduction, diminishment, or restriction through a series of nightly progressions leading to completion at the dark moon. It's also a good time to use magic to help fortify your resolve to carry out any personal improvement goals that involve cutting back on or quitting a harmful habit.

THIRD-QUARTER/WANING HALF MOON: This phase of the moon when it has diminished from a full moon back to a half moon is useful for organizing and clarifying. It is also a good time for magic intended to bring decisiveness or endings, or to help straighten out entangled and confusing situations.

 BALSAMIC MOON/WANING CRESCENT: While the waning crescent phase includes the time from the third quarter (waning half moon) to the time of the dark moon, the term *balsamic moon* is usually used to describe the very last sliver of visible moon, seen only briefly before dawn in the days just before the dark moon. This is a good time for magic to aid in letting go, and for finalizing banishing spells and ongoing purification magic. The balsamic moon has a healing, soothing energy flow that can be drawn on to bring comfort to those in need.

Moonrise and Moonset

Just as magic can be timed to coincide with sunrise and sunset, so too can the rising and setting of the moon provide excellent canvases on which to craft your spells. As the moon rises above the horizon, we may think about our magical intentions also rising upwards, transiting through the heavens. As the moon sets, we might think about our will being set, our magic being sealed, our spell being delivered, and our intentions locked in place as the moon disappears from our view. There are many apps and online resources you can use to determine the exact times of moonrise and moonset at your location, but awareness of vsome basics is helpful as well. The moon rises and sets at predictable times corresponding to the lunar phase:

- The new moon rises and sets with the sun.
- For each day following the new moon, the time of moonrise and moonset lags approximately fifty minutes behind the sun.

- The first quarter waxing half moon rises around local noon (the point where the sun crosses the meridian, or midway point) and sets around local midnight (twelve hours after local noon).
- The full moon rises around sunset and sets around sunrise.
- The third quarter waning half moon rises around local midnight and sets around local noon.

You might also notice that the position of moonrise and moonset shifts in accordance with the changing seasons. In the winter in the Northern Hemisphere, the full moon rises in the northeast, and the new moon rises in the southeast. In the summer, these positions are reversed, with the full moon rising in the southeast, and the new moon rising in the northeast. In the spring and fall, the full moon and new moon both rise nearer to due east, while the rising and setting positions of the quarter moons take on a southerly or northerly bent. In the spring, the first quarter moon (waxing half moon) rises in the northeast while the third quarter moon (waning half moon) rises in the southeast. In the autumn, the first quarter moon rises in the southeast while the third quarter moon rises in the northeast.

If you're planning to link your magic to the rising or setting of the moon, time your ritual to take place as closely to the time of moonrise or moonset as possible. Face the direction in which the moon is rising or setting as you work your magic. Even if the action of the moon's rising or setting is not visible to you, you can still draw on the moon's energies by thinking of its presence and position in relation to the earth. If you're working with the moonrise, you might think of the earth rotating on its axis, bringing the moon into view from your own little corner of the earth as you project your magic onto this new outlook, into this new window of possibility. If you're working with the moonset, you might think of the turning earth as a lock clicking into place, sealing your intention as the moon dips below the horizon.

The Moon's Day and Hour

In classical astrology, each day of the week is assigned to one of the seven luminaries, the celestial bodies that we can see moving through the skies without the aid of a telescope: the sun for Sunday, the moon for Monday, Mars for Tuesday, Mercury for Wednesday, Jupiter for

Thursday, Venus for Friday, and Saturn for Saturday. The hours of the day are similarly distinguished, with the hours of sunrise and sunset belonging to the ruling luminary of the day, and the other hours following a repeating sequence of the seven luminaries. While the moon is the overall ruler of Monday, the other luminaries have their own hours on Monday as well, just as the moon has its own special hours that occur during each of the seven days of the week. There are different and somewhat overlapping systems for calculating the planetary hours. You can find sources online that describe the various methods of calculation. If you would rather avoid the technicalities, just keep in mind that on each planet's day, the ruling luminary rules not only that entire day, but in particular the sunrise and sunset hours of that day.

When planning a moon spell, you might decide to do your casting during one of the hours ruled by the moon, or on the moon's day, Monday. Doing so can help boost the power of your spell as the lunar energies are believed to have a magnified influence on the earth during these times. While it's not necessary to time your magic in accordance with the planetary hours and days, doing so can give your spells a bit of extra power and a better chance for success.

LUNAR DISTANCES

The moon is on average approximately 238,855 miles from Earth. That means 30 Earth-sized planets could fit in between Earth and the moon.

Walking 3 miles an hour 24 hours a day 7 days a week, you could walk the distance from Earth to the moon in a little over 7 years.

The moon's circumference is 6,786 miles, which is equal to only about 2.3 times the distance from NYC to San Francisco.

The Moon in the Signs of the Zodiac

Another option is to time your moon spells to take best advantage of the moon's monthly movement through the twelve signs of the zodiac. Imagine an invisible circle stretching beyond the earth and extending in all directions, and imagine that circle divided up into twelve equal portions, each portion representing 30 degrees of the 360 degrees that comprise the whole circle. This is the geocentric or earth-centered zodiac. Each of the twelve portions of this imaginary circle represents one of the twelve signs of the zodiac, and as the moon circles the earth, it moves through each of these signs in turn, spending about two and a half days in each sign. Each zodiac sign is believed to impart its own qualities and characteristics, and thus each sign is considered to be beneficial to certain activities, and detrimental to other activities. By timing your lunar magic to coincide with the moon being in a favorable sign for your particular magical working, you'll know that the general flow of vibrations will be conducive to manifesting your aim. You can certainly cast a lunar spell at any time, regardless of what sign of the zodiac the moon is passing through, but you will encounter fewer challenges if you work with the general flow of energies rather than against it. Noting the moon's movement through the zodiac gives us yet another way to read the energies of the day, so that we can plan our endeavors to utilize and enjoy each moment to its full potential.

Astrology is an art and a science that has many layers and aspects into which you can dive as deep as you wish. There's not only the moon's movement to consider but also the position of the planets as well. Each planet has its own qualities as does each sign of the zodiac. The angles and aspects that the planets make with one another as they move through their orbits may also be taken into account. One might also consider how the current lunar and planetary positions relate to the personal natal chart, an astrological snapshot of where the planets and moon and sun were in relation to the earth at a person's exact time and location of birth. To get the full and complete picture, one would need to weigh the combined effects of all of these different influences.

Astrology can get very complicated and complex very quickly! Fortunately, though, it doesn't require a deep study to take advantage of many aspects of astrological timing. Here are some ideas to consider to enable you to take advantage of the moon's monthly movement through the signs of the zodiac; you can consult online sources or

Llewellyn's *Moon Sign Book* to find out in which sign the moon is currently located:

♈ **MOON IN ARIES:** Aries is ruled by the planet Mars. This sign imparts an eager, aggressive energy that may lead to rash actions and conflicts, but it also lends itself well to endeavors requiring leadership, assertiveness, and courage. The moon in Aries is a good time for casting spells to boost courage, increase energy, or enhance your leadership abilities. It's also a good time for defensive and protective spellwork, as well as ambitious spellwork that requires a greater than usual level of boldness and power.

♉ **MOON IN TAURUS:** Taurus is ruled by Venus. Taurus imparts a reliable, stable energy that can be a bit stubborn. The moon in Taurus is a good time for casting spells for courage, determination, ambition, friendship, love, balance, or stability. When the moon is in Taurus, choose spells that go with the flow and that don't rock the boat or upset the status quo too much, as energies may be more resistant to change at this time.

Ⅱ **MOON IN GEMINI:** Gemini is ruled by the planet Mercury. Gemini brings alertness, mental sharpness, and an adventurous, fun-loving quality, but it can also be dualistic and a little undependable. The moon in Gemini offers a good time for magic that takes risks or brings progress or adventure. It's also a good time for spellwork meant to bring peace, sympathy, mental clarity, and new ideas and solutions.

♋ **MOON IN CANCER:** Cancer is ruled by the moon. Cancer brings a creative, healing, compassionate, and nurturing energy, but can also be a bit sensitive, sorrowful, and withdrawn. The moon in Cancer is a good time for spellwork meant to heal the emotions, bring comfort, encourage inspiration, increase creativity, and support success in creative or artistic endeavors. It's also a good time for spells intended to protect the home and family, as well as for magic to strengthen emotional bonds and attachments.

♌ **MOON IN LEO:** Leo is ruled by the sun. Leo imparts charisma, confidence, persistence, and assertiveness, and it has a fun-loving, gregarious spirit that demands attention and seeks the spotlight. The moon in Leo is a good time for ambitious spellwork, magic to boost confidence, and spells to support self-reliance. It's also a good time for magic to bring success, encourage leadership, strengthen perseverance, increase loyalty, encourage generosity, increase charisma, attract friends, and gain admiration.

Turn over the change in your pockets at the new moon to attract more money.

♍ MOON IN VIRGO: Virgo is ruled by Mercury. Virgo imparts a discerning, analytical quality that is great for organizing and for solving problems, but there can be an overly critical tendency toward perfectionism. The moon in Virgo is a good time for spellwork to bring clarity or solve problems. It's also good for spells intended to support talent, increase ambition, hone skills, manifest travel opportunities, or to bring moderation and reserve.

MOON IN LIBRA: Libra is ruled by Venus. Libra brings balance and imparts a diplomatic, cooperative spirit that encourages teamwork and harmonious relationships. This sign can be a bit indecisive. The moon in Libra is a good time for magic to improve relationships, attract partners, increase abundance, boost popularity, ease troubles, encourage love, bring peace, or encourage cooperation and favorable negotiations. It's also a good time for spellwork meant to bring balance.

MOON IN SCORPIO: Scorpio is ruled by Pluto. Scorpio brings a powerful, intense, determined, excitable energy that seeks solutions and encourages enterprise. There can be a tendency toward impulsiveness and aggression. The moon in Scorpio is good for magic to bring quick action, improve ability, boost courage and confidence, and increase success. It's also a good sign for strengthening attachments, uncovering hidden truths, and bringing about revolutions to outmoded power structures.

MOON IN SAGITTARIUS: Sagittarius is ruled by Jupiter. Sagittarius has an enthusiastic, expansive energy that brings luck and encouragement. There is a generous, charitable spirit but also a quickness and restlessness that can lead to rashness. The moon in Sagittarius is a good time for spells to encourage kindness and generosity, increase enthusiasm, bring happiness, achieve goals, bring forgiveness, increase optimism, and bring about changes. It's also a good sign for travel magic and for magic to bring good luck.

MOON IN CAPRICORN: Capricorn is ruled by Saturn. Capricorn brings a calculating and ambitious energy that supports leadership and favors those in authority. It has an objective, careful quality that is good for bringing structure and moderation. There can be a certain tendency toward shying away from emotional matters. The moon in Capricorn is a good time for spellwork to bring structure, encourage responsibility, gain interest, improve leadership, increase ambition, bring respect, encourage frugality or moderation, and boost confidence.

≈ **MOON IN AQUARIUS:** Aquarius is ruled by Uranus. Aquarius has a rebellious, intelligent, expansive energy that favors innovation, revolution, and unconventional approaches. Its energies can be a bit fanatical, intense, and scattered. The moon in Aquarius is a good time for magic to bring about revolution, change, and innovation, spells for expansion, spells to encourage new perspectives and new ways of being, spells to bring freedom and independence, spells with idealistic or visionary aims, and magic that takes an unconventional or unusual approach.

⟩⟨ **MOON IN PISCES:** Pisces is ruled by Neptune. Pisces imparts a dreamy, imaginative, peaceful, artistic, laid-back energy that encourages inspiration, romance, and creativity. It can be a bit impractical and restless. The moon in Pisces is a good time for magic to encourage creativity, improve artistic skills, encourage kindness, attract romance, encourage love, or increase beauty. It's also good for psychic work and for magic to increase intuition.

It's Always Time for
Moon Magic Somewhere!

There are other systems of lunar timing that you can investigate and utilize, including the Indian lunar mansions, Arabic lunar mansions, Chinese lunar mansions, and the Western house system. It should be noted that wherever the moon and whatever its phase, you can find a way to create a spell that takes into account those influences and makes the most of them. The moon's movement through the heavens doesn't limit the type of goals you might choose to pursue in your magical workings at any given time, but it can inform the angle of approach you take in your spellcrafting so that your magic has an easier time doing what's intended. For instance, if your goal is to accumulate wealth so that you can buy a house, if the moon is waxing you might cast a spell for increasing income, whereas if the moon is waning you might cast a spell to diminish debts or curb spending.

Chapter Four

LUNAR POTIONS AND POWDERS

In this chapter, you'll learn how to make many different types of lunar potions and powders that can improve psychic ability, enhance beauty, protect against enemies, encourage good feelings, hasten the action of spells, and more. Powders are mixtures of primarily dry ingredients and potions are mixtures of primarily liquid ingredients, chosen and blended with specific magical effects in mind. In the case of lunar powders and potions, ingredients may be chosen for their lunar attributes or activated and enchanted by the power of the moon. One advantage of using potions and powders in your magic is that they offer a discreet spellcasting medium. You might sprinkle a powder or potion around the perimeter of a building or even around a whole city to effect a change on the space and its occupants without anyone being the wiser. Potions and powders are also versatile, effective, and easy to use. You might anoint a candle with a lunar potion attuned to your intention, or sprinkle a small bit of powder on a candle flame to add a literal spark to your magical working. You might spread out a powder in the shape of a symbol that encapsulates the goal of your spell, or use a potion to trace a magical symbol on your body to help awaken your higher powers. Lunar potions and powders can be simple or complex, depending on your preferences and purpose. Make your lunar formulations at night whenever possible, and charge them up with the energy of the moon.

Potions and Powders Basics

There are a few basic rules of making potions and powders that you should always adhere to … some obvious, others easily overlooked or forgotten. The most important rule is to never use any toxic, unknown, or synthetic ingredients in any potions or powders that are intended to be ingested or used on the skin. Also, be sure to keep any potions or powders that contain such ingredients out of the reach of children and pets, and this includes keeping any items that have been anointed or sprinkled with such formulations out of reach, as well. If you want to make a potion that you can drink or a powder you can eat, play it safe and choose only food-grade ingredients that you have ingested before without any negative consequences. Please note also that some stones and crystals contain toxic minerals such as lead or sulfur that can leach into any liquid they are placed in—never ingest such a potion even if the stones or crystals have been removed. If you're making a potion or powder to be used on the skin, avoid using any potentially toxic ingredients, and avoid using any ingredients that are potential skin irritants. Avoid synthetic oils, and be sure to dilute any essential oils such as cinnamon oil or peppermint oil that can cause irritation if used undiluted. If you're pregnant or planning to get pregnant, or if you take any medications, be sure to check with your doctor before using any potions or powders internally or externally that contain essential oils or herbs you're not sure about, as many common ingredients can have an abortifacient effect. Please note also that babies and small children can be particularly sensitive to certain herbs and essential oils, so keep your potions and powders safely away from them. Don't let your potions and powders sit around too long, and toss them out if they develop a strange or stale odor or unusual appearance. Store your lunar potions and powders out of direct sunlight to preserve their power until ready for use. You can use opaque containers, wrap clear containers in fabric, or simply store your concoctions in a drawer or cabinet to keep them out of the light. Finally, take care to keep your utensils, mortar and pestle, mixing bowls or cauldron clean; you don't want yesterday's spellwork to contaminate today's magic.

Containers and Utensils

You'll find in the potion and powder recipes in this chapter suggestions for the ideal types of containers in which to store and mix each potion. These suggestions are based on the magical qualities of different materials as well as the vibrational energies of various colors. However, you might not always have such containers on hand. This is no reason to worry or delay your magic-making. Especially if you're going to be using the formulation right away instead of storing it, virtually any container will do in a pinch. As long as it's clean and will hold your potion or powder, it's a suitable container. Your own magical abilities are enough to make up for any shortcomings in the containers you use. However, it certainly doesn't hurt to give your potions and powders the most power possible! Try to choose containers that correspond with the intention and energies of the recipe you're using whenever possible, but don't stress it if you don't have just the right thing. Be aware though that the longer you plan to store the potion or powder, the choice of container becomes more significant as you have to think about sunlight and air exposure, contamination, and other concerns. If you use the formulation quickly, however, it should still work fine no matter what sort of container you put it in.

Here are some tips to help you choose the best container and mixing utensils for your lunar potions and powders:

- Avoid plastic if possible, as it has a very dull vibration that seems to interfere with magical energies.

- Opaque containers will better protect your potion or powder from sunlight.

- Containers made from natural materials that harmonize with your magical goal are ideal. For storing or mixing a lunar potion or powder, look for containers made of silver, moonstone, crystal, or glass, or go traditional and mix your blends in an iron cauldron.

- What you stir or crush your concoction with can also add or subtract power. A long crystal, a wand, an ordinary stick, a wooden spoon, or a silver spoon make good stirring utensils for lunar potions, while a silver knife or a mortar and pestle made of crystal, jade, or a black-colored stone will prove useful for making lunar powders.

- If your recipe is to be heated, you will need to make sure all your mixing containers and utensils are heatproof and safe to use as cookware. Some pottery glazes give off toxic fumes when heated, so don't take any chances.

- Take care that any heated formulation has cooled sufficiently before transferring it into another container that could potentially melt or shatter.

- If you don't want to invest in fancy containers, ordinary mason jars or empty wine bottles, spaghetti sauce jars, or baby food jars work just fine. You can wrap fabric around the outside of the container to protect the mixture from sunlight and to add color symbolism and pizazz. Powders can be wrapped in fabric or even kept in envelopes if you don't happen to have a jar handy.

Lunar Potions

While a lunar potion can be as simple as a mixture of moonlight and water, other ingredients such as herbs, stones, and essential oils can be added to increase the efficacy of the potion and to make it more specific to your unique intention. Spring water, rain water, well water, and water collected at night from a natural source all make good base liquids for a lunar potion, as does lemon juice, coconut water, coconut milk, cherry juice, peach juice, or apricot juice. Let the recipes offered here inspire your own adventures in lunar potion-making.

• • • POTION 1 • • •
Full Moon Potion

This full moon potion can be used in an impressive variety of applications. The recipe below results in a powerful

potion that resonates with the qualities of psychic awareness, magical power, amplification, manifestation, and illumination. Use it to anoint your ritual tools, divination tools,
or ritual space to enhance psychic abilities and magnify
magical power, or utilize it to strengthen spells intended to
manifest resources, bring clarity, attract love, increase luck,
or achieve success. This potion can also be used as a base
potion to which you may add other harmonious ingredients
and elements. It should be made on the night of the full
moon, after the moon has risen and the sun has set.

Fill a silver bowl or cauldron with water collected
from a natural source. Place it so that you can see the
reflection of the full moon shining in the water. Hold a
clear quartz crystal in your hand and feel its radiating
energy. Imagine this energy stretching out and reaching
up toward the moon. Feel yourself connected to this
thread of energy, and envision your own power magnifying as you reach up toward the moon with the crystal in
your hand. Drop the crystal into the water. Next, do the
same process with a moonstone. Hold the stone in your
hand and feel its distinct yet equally potent power. Think
of the stone's connection to the moonlight, and imagine your own energies weaving around this connecting
thread, stretching all the way up to the moon and fun-

neling its luminescence and power back down into the stone and into your own body. Place the moonstone in the water.

Stir the potion clockwise as you envision the moon's energy flowing down into the mixture. If you like, speak the following verse or communicate your intention with your own words of power:

> Water, moonstone, crystal clear,
> call the moonlight, bring it here!
> Gather here its glowing light;
> gather here its awesome sight!
> Gather here its growing might!
> Gather here its magic bright!
> Lady Luna, on this night,
> please share with me your magic light!

Bottle up the potion right away in a silver or crystal container. You can leave the stones in the potion or remove them. Store this potion in a dark, cool place, away from direct sunlight.

Press a moonstone to your lips as you gaze at the full moon to bring a vision of the future.

Dark Moon Potion

This dark moon potion has magical energies that can be used to hide or hinder, to banish or bind. Use it to anoint spell implements used in magical operations for which you want to cover your tracks so as to render the origin of the magic untraceable, or use it to anoint your body if you're wishing to go unnoticed and avoid attracting attention for whatever reason. You can also use it to help strengthen banishing and binding magic, and as an aid to spirit communication and dream work. Like the full moon potion, this dark moon potion can also be adapted to more specific intentions with additional ingredients such as stones and herbs. Make this potion on a night of the dark moon, before the moon again becomes visible in its waxing form.

Fill a black, opaque container with water collected at night from rainfall or from a pond, lake, or other natural water source. Dig a hole in the ground deep enough to envelop your potion bottle or simply pile soil around the sides of the bottle for a similar effect. Leave the top of the bottle open and exposed to the night sky. Feel the darkness surrounding you, and see if you can find a feeling of peace in the stillness of the night. Think of the energies of the dark moon—healing, protecting, concealing, purifying, nourishing, transforming—and invite these essences to enter into your potion. Drop into the potion bottle a piece of onyx, a piece of obsidian, and a piece of smoky quartz. You can use this verse to accompany this action, dropping in a stone with each stanza:

Dark moon!

Hidden moon!

Secret and concealing moon!

Protective, safe, and healing moon!

Cleansing and transforming moon!

Enter here and give me sight,

in shadows deep, devoid of light!

Keep me safe and hold me near,

Keep my pathway crystal clear!

Leave the potion in the ground for a few hours, but retrieve it before sunrise. Close the container before you pull it up out of the ground, then keep it wrapped in black cloth or stored in a dark space.

PLANTING BY THE MOON

Farmers have been planting crops according to the moon phase for ages, and you can do the same when gardening. Plants such as flowers, peas, and tomatoes that bear fruit above the ground should be planted during the waxing moon. Plants such as carrots, potatoes, and peanuts that bear fruit beneath the ground should be planted during the waning moon.

How does it work? Just as the moon affects tides, it also affects things like the water content of soil and the gravitational pull on roots.

Waxing Moon Potion

Try this waxing moon potion in spells intended to manifest success and growth. Use it to anoint spell candles for an extra boost of power or to quicken the effects of a magical working. Mix this potion anytime during the moon's waxing phase.

Break up a small piece of selenite using a mortar and pestle. Add a vanilla bean, and continue to mash and blend the ingredients. Place the powdered mixture into a silver container and add some spring water. Place the container outside, preferably in an area where it's surrounded by vegetation. Invite the energies of the waxing moon into the potion as you envision the moonlight mixing in with the blend, imparting its magical qualities. Using your wand, a silver spoon, or a crystal, stir the potion clockwise thirteen times as you visualize growth and increase, perhaps imagining a growing mountain of gold coins, or a field of plants growing larger and larger and blooming overnight. Leave the potion outside for a while but retrieve it before sunrise. Keep the potion in a silver, blue, or white container.

Waning Moon Potion

This potion is good for restoring balance and encouraging moderation. It's also a powerful addition to spells intended to diminish, reduce, temper, or weaken. Mix this potion during a waning moon any time after the moon has reached its third quarter phase. Choose a dark gray or black container and fill it to the top with spring water. Take this container outside and hold it skyward. Imagine in your mind's eye the waning moon's reduction and how the energies shift during this time. Ponder how the moon transforms from a state of intense luminosity to a state of obscurity and invisibility yet is ever-present and essentially unchanging throughout this endless cycle. Invite the energies of the waning moon to enter into the potion. Stir the potion counterclockwise thirteen times with a slightly curved, dark-colored stick as you envision the moon reducing in size and think of tides receding, waves softening, curtains being drawn across a window to filter and diminish the glaring light. Pour out a small amount of the potion and cap it up. Wrap it up in a dark gray or black cloth and keep it away from direct sunlight.

Truth-Revealing Potion

This potion can be used to bring light to situations involving hidden elements or dishonesties, revealing what is obscured and uncovering significant missing pieces. Create it at the time of the new moon, after the waxing crescent has reappeared.

Just after sunset when you can see the new moon sinking toward the horizon, light a white candle and think of this light connecting to the light of the new moon. Pour some spring water into a heat-proof container, and hold this over the candle to warm the water. Think about the light and heat from the candle flame and the light from the new moon flowing into the water, infusing it with magical power. Add a red, a white, and a yellow rose petal to the water as you consider the information that you would like revealed. Add a pinch of sea salt as you imagine any deceptions or concealments dissolving away. Gently swirl the potion, visualizing how the new moon's crescent of light will grow larger and larger over the coming days. Imagine that as the moon's light grows, the veil concealing the truth will also be peeled back to reveal the answers and information you seek. If you like, chant this verse as you mix the potion:

chapter four

All that is hidden from me tonight,

will be revealed by the moon's bright light!

Show to me, moon, with your all-seeing sight,

the truth that I seek on this new moon night.

Before the moon's full circle glows,

the truth revealed, the hidden shown!

I'll know all that I need to know,

as the moon reveals her growing glow!

You can use the potion to anoint an artifact or symbol of the situation (for example, copies of legal documents if the matter involves a court case), or dab it on objects that the person from whom you wish to compel the truth is likely to touch.

• • • POTION 6 • • •
Beauty Potion

This simple lunar potion can be used to enhance beauty and renew one's youthful qualities. When conditions are favorable for dew to form in your area and the moon is in a waxing phase, head outside before dawn to an area with a lot of grass or other ground-level vegetation. Bring a washcloth sized piece of organic cotton, hemp, or another absorbent fabric. Gently drag the fabric over the dew-covered plants, then wring out the liquid into a large-mouthed jar. If you prefer, you can skip the fabric and attempt to coax the dew from the plants straight into the jar, but it's a much more time-consuming and tedious method if you're hoping to collect a decent amount. Once you've collected the dew, place within the jar a moonstone. Swirl the potion as you envision yourself shining with an inner beauty that permeates through your outer form as well. Dip your fingertips into the potion and place some on your face, hands, elbows, knees, neck, chest—anywhere you wish to enhance your beauty and revitalize your outward appearance. Store the potion in a silver container away from sunlight, and use it only at night for best results.

• • •

Lunar Powders

While magical powders are typically thought of as finely textured blends of dried herbs and powdered stones, the term can be applied more loosely to include mixtures of fresh herbs, barks, soil, and other chunkier or somewhat moist, solid ingredients. Powders can come in many textures and they can include many ingredients such as small bits of fabric or money, or small amounts of essential oils. As long as the resulting mixture can be spread or sprinkled about easily, anything goes as far as ingredient choices for your magical powder blends. Rich soil, graveyard dirt, poppy seeds, and vanilla powder are among the many ingredients that might be used as a base for a lunar powder. After you read through the recipes here, try to think of a few other lunar powder blends you might create for different magical purposes.

• • • POWDER 1 • • •
Love Powder

This powder resonates with a loving, soft, romantic, and attractive energy. Use this powder in spells to attract love and romance, carry it with you in a sachet to bring new potential partners your way, or sprinkle it in a place where you spend time with your lover to strengthen an existing relationship.

Place a large handful of dried rose petals into a silver, clear, or blue bowl. Add to this the pits of three cherries and a few drops of jasmine oil. Blend the mixture together under the light of the moon as you think of your desire for love and romance and envision the moonlight flowing into the mixture. Let your intentions mingle with the herbs and with the undeniable pull and attraction of the moon.

Create a feeling of overwhelming love and passion in your heart and send it up toward the moon. Envision this energy bounding back off the moon in a magnified form, shining rays of loving power into your magical blend. Keep the powder in a pouch or sachet of red, blue, purple, or white cloth, or store it in a clear, blue, or silver container.

• • • POWDER 2 • • •
Spirit Powder

Use this powder to help open the channels of communication between the living and the dead. Sprinkle it onto spirit communication tools such as spirit boards and pendulums to attract spirits and enhance mediumship abilities, or place some on your altar during rituals to call upon or honor the dead.

Mix together a handful of crushed mugwort, a pinch of sage, a pinch of violet flowers or leaves, a pinch of cannabis flower or hemp seeds, and a mushroom. Break the mixture down into smaller pieces as you think of the energies of the ingredients blending to create a powder that will open a gateway into the world of spirit. You can use this verse to charge the powder with the power of the moon, or speak your own words that describe the effects you would like the powder to produce:

Keeper of the cauldron!

Mother of the dead!

Grant me access to those who have come before me!

Open the way, so that I may speak with the dead!

Between the worlds, let me walk with honor!

Between the worlds, I will walk with respect!

Keeper of the cauldron!

Mother of the dead!

Open the way and put that way into this powder!

Great Goddess, please grant me

the power to speak with the dead!

Leave the mixture outside under the moonlight for a few hours, and retrieve it before sunrise. Keep the powder in a black, opaque container or wrapped in a black cloth. Store it near photos of your ancestors, or keep it near the fireplace or in a hidden, dark location.

• • • POWDER 3 • • •
Protection Powder

This powder offers a protective, defensive, shielding energy. Use it to add power to protective and defensive spellwork, tie it up in a sachet and carry it with you for extra protection, or sprinkle it around your magic space or across the threshold of your property to create an invisible barrier to help keep away any unwanted arrivals.

Mix together a handful of black pepper, a handful of sea salt, nine juniper berries, a small piece of bark from an elm tree, and several thorns from a hawthorn tree (gathered from the ground, not plucked off the tree). Crush the ingredients with a mortar and pestle as you think of the moon's strength and power, its influence and authority over life systems here on earth. Chant this verse as you crush and mix the ingredients:

The moon is my scythe;

the moon is my shield!

It's the moon up above whose power I wield!

All enemies scatter; no dangers come near.

All worries are shattered; no dangers to fear.

The moon is my scythe;

the moon is my shield.

The moon is the light whose power I wield!

Keep the powder in a black or white opaque container or cloth, and store it out of sight.

• • • POWDER 4 • • •
• • • POWDER 4 • • •
Dreams and Divination Powder

Use this blend to help open the psychic senses and heighten your awareness of the astral realms. Rub your hands in the mixture before doing divination, or place some in a sachet under your pillow to encourage prophetic or lucid dreaming.

In a black bowl, mix together a pinch of poppy seeds and a pinch of red rose petals. Add to this some small pieces of serpentine and a piece of amethyst. Place this outside under the moonlight. Hold your hand above the bowl and gaze at the moon then at the bowl, willing the energies of the moon to enter into the herbs. You can use this verse to help convey your intention:

> Illuminate! Enlighten!
>
> Absorb the moon and brighten!
>
> Shine your light within the dark!
>
> Show me all within your spark!
>
> In the shadows, let me walk!
>
> Illuminate! Enlighten!

Leave this outside for several hours, then store it in an opaque purple or black container or cloth.

Cheering Powder

Use this blend to help bring a spirit of fun and frivolity, mischief and play. Place it in a sachet or sprinkle it around the area where you would like to encourage goodwill and good times, or use it when freshly made as an edible topping for cookies or cakes to help imbue those who eat it with a feeling of joy.

Mix together a handful of coconut flakes with a tablespoon of lemon zest. As you mix the ingredients, think of the moon shining down on a scene of fun and wild abandonment. You might imagine a menagerie of animals frolicking in a moonlit clearing in the middle of a forest, or you might envision you and your friends dancing wildly under a starry sky and glowing moon. Fill your heart with the emotions of good times and happiness; let a carefree spirit overcome you. Smile as you blend together the coconut and lemon zest with the emotionally charged energies of your thoughts. Use this verse to call the energies of the moon into the mixture, or simply stir with intention as you gaze at the moon and think of those energies coming into the blend:

Moon so bright,

please come and play!

Make us happy, make us gay!

Fill us with your shining light!

Moon so joyful, moon so bright!

If you intend to eat this mixture, do so right away, when the ingredients are fresh and the magic is at its most vibrant. If you're going to use it in another way and would like to store it, place it in a white or silver container and add a clear quartz crystal to help keep the magical energies active.

• • •

Chapter Five

MOON SPELLS
BY LUNAR PHASE

This chapter includes a selection of spells arranged by the lunar phase in which they should be cast. You'll find spells to practice during the waxing moon and waning moon, and at the full moon and dark moon. If you see a spell here that interests you but the moon isn't in the recommended phase, consult the chapter on lunar timing for inspiration, and adapt the magic as you see fit. For instance, waning moon spells can be easily adapted to coincide with a setting moon, while waxing moon spells can be adapted to synchronize with the moonrise. Challenge yourself to think of other magic you might perform during these lunar phases in addition to the spells suggested here.

Waxing Moon Magic

As we witness the moon's light grow from a thin crescent into a full circle, we have a visual representation of growth, increase, illumination, and the completion of cycles. By linking our everyday activities and endeavors to the energies and symbolism of the waxing moon, we can ride the natural wave of vibrations to surround our goals with the same energies of increase and expansion, growth and abundance.

• • • SPELL 1 • • •
Waxing Moon Spell for Increase and Success

Cast this spell during a waxing moon to bring general increase and success to your endeavors. Place on your lunar altar or outside under the moonlight an item or symbol to represent the area of your life where you wish to bring more success or increase. If you want to bring success to your love life, you might choose a symbol of a heart. If you want to increase your productivity at work, you might choose an item that represents the type of work you do. Circle around the item you have chosen, skipping, walking with a purposeful stride, or dancing. Alternatively, you might simply trace a circle around the item with your fingertip or wand. Call down the power of the moon and raise the energy as much as you can as you make your way around the circle. Make thirteen complete rotations around the item, and think of your success growing and increasing with each rotation. Stand before the item and place your hands on it as you envision the moon waxing to full. Send the energy you have raised into the item. Use this verse to seal the spell:

Magical moon,

Grow fat and wide!

Bring me success as you bring in the tide!

Increase in abundance, magical light!

Nourish and grow what I wish for tonight!

• • • SPELL 2 • • •
Waxing Moon Spell to Reveal the Truth

If you feel that something is being hidden from you that you would like to know, try this spell during a waxing moon. Write down on a small piece of paper a description of the situation, a statement of the information you would like to know, and a list of names of whoever is arousing your suspicions. Take this paper outside when the moon is visible. Read the words you have written as if you are telling the moon about your troubles. If you have tarot cards and wish to further strengthen the spell, lay the paper down on top of the Moon tarot card. If you don't have a tarot deck, place the paper on the bare ground or on a black cloth. Take a pinch of bay leaves in your hand and think about pulling the moonlight down into the herbs that rest in your hand. Feel the energies in the bay change to a different vibration as the lunar power is incorporated. Rub the bay leaves all over the surface of the paper as you say this spell and envision the truth you wish to know coming to light just as the waxing moon's light will grow:

> The truth revealed! The truth revealed!
> What's hidden cannot stay concealed!
> I am the moon that shines on all!
> I am the moon that stands so tall!
> I see you sneak, I see you crawl!
> You cannot hide, or you will fall!
> Tonight, you tell the truth to all!
> May hidden actions be revealed,
> and secret thoughts no more concealed!

Your tongue is loose, your lips unsealed!
Reveal to me! The truth be spilled!

Fold the bay leaves up in the paper to make a small packet, then carry this with you, place it on your altar, or put it somewhere hidden in a location where the suspicious party is likely to spend time, or where the suspicious activity is likely to occur. Once you find out what you are wanting to know, you can recycle the paper and scatter the bay leaves outside.

• • • SPELL 3 • • •

Waxing Moon Spell for Wealth

Use this spell to increase your wealth, whether you desire monetary wealth or a less tangible form of treasure and abundance. Take your wallet or purse outside under the light of a waxing moon. Be sure it has some money in it already, even if it's only just a few coins. Take a moment to think about what work you do in the universe. How do you serve the earth and/or your fellow humans? You might serve others through your profession or contribute to the world in other ways. Whatever you consider to be your most important work, whatever energy you are willing to expend for the benefit of the world at large, think now about these efforts. Envision the effort

To move into a new house during a waxing moon is said to invite prosperity.

and work that you do spreading out from your heart center, touching lives, transforming the earth. Imagine this work that you do being sent out into the universe, then imagine that flow reflecting off the moon and returning to you as wealth in many forms. Hold your wallet or purse aloft toward the sky, opening it up to catch the stream of moonlight and wealth coming to you. Repeat this process each night through the full moon, adding more coins to your purse or wallet on each successive night. Think about what wealth means to you as well as the wealth that you bring to the world. Reaffirm your intentions and resolve. If you like, you can incorporate this verse:

I vow to you,
bright moon above,
to do my work in light and love!
What I send forth, bring back to me,
in wealth, in gold, in currency!

By the growing moon, by the bountiful sea,

great wealth to me, come!

So mote it be!

Full Moon Charging Ritual

The full moon is a wonderful time to charge ritual tools or other objects you use mystically or magically. Such tools and objects might include crystals and other stones, tarot decks, a magic wand, a cauldron, candles, or even special garments and jewelry that you wear for meditation or magic. "Charging" is another word for "empower." You might think of it as activation, as you are literally turning on and fine-tuning various capabilities and actions of the item.

On a white or silver cloth, place the item you wish to charge with the full moon's energies. Arrange thirteen moonstones around the object in a circular or elliptical pattern. Focus your mind on the moon, and invite the energies from that heavenly body to flow into your space and into the object to be charged. If you like, place your hand on the object and chant:

I dedicate you to the moon!

Fulfill your purpose! Be in tune!

(repeat three times)

Wrap the moonstones and the object together in a soft cloth of celestial blue, silver, purple, or white. Keep the bundle wrapped up and in a dark space for a few days so that the object can further absorb energies from the moonstones and attune to these vibrations.

• • • OTHER MAGIC 3 • • •
Full Moon Dedication

If you are wanting extra assurance that you will stay committed to a particular promise or purpose, this dedication oath sealed by the full moon will not only open the way, but will also help you to stay on course. You'll need a small piece of the best quality paper you have. Ordinary notebook or typing paper will do, but it might be more aesthetically appealing to you if you choose a nicer paper. You might even choose to go all-out and create your own paper from recycled scraps. You can find instructions and tutorials for this fairly simple process online.

Take the paper and a pen to a place where you can see the full moon glowing brightly. Write on the paper a statement expressing your oath. You might begin with a simple, "I will___," filling in the blank with whatever purpose or promise you are determined to fulfill. Place the paper in front of you with the words facing upwards toward the sky. Use these words or compose your own verse of similar effect:

I make this oath in full view of the powers of nature!

May the full moon bear witness as I make this oath!

May the full moon bear witness to my dedicated heart and mind!

As I will myself to be, then so I am!

As the moon stays its course, so too will I!

Now speak the words of your written oath as if you are promising it directly to the moon. Roll the paper into a scroll and tie it with a red thread or ribbon. Keep this scroll somewhere safe, hidden, and private, perhaps tucking it inside a little pouch or treasure box you can stash in a trunk or drawer. Take it out and hold the scroll in your hands whenever you need extra encouragement to remain committed to whatever it is you have promised yourself to do.

• • •

LUNAR DEITIES

Deities associated with the moon have been revered since ancient times. In Mesopotamia, a god called Nanna, or Sin, was worshipped as a lunar god who had the power to provide resources and encourage unity. In west Africa in the ancient kingdom of Dahomey, Mawu was celebrated as a lunar goddess presiding over creation, birth, fertility, abundance, and inspiration. Selene was a lunar goddess known to the ancient Greeks, while the ancient Romans honored the goddess Luna. In the Americas, the Oceti Sakowin celebrated Hanwi, a protective lunar goddess whose name translates as "night sun." Today, the moon continues to inspire many people around the world.

Waning Moon Magic

As the moon's light diminishes from a full circle back to a tiny sliver that soon disappears entirely out of view, we have a ready symbol of reduction, banishment, and concealment that can be utilized in our magical workings to achieve a vast variety of effects. By harmonizing our spellwork with the energies of the waning moon, we find a way to cast aside what no longer serves us, a way to bring endings and closures, a way to sneak through the shadows unnoticed.

• • • SPELL 4 • • •

Waning Moon Banishing Spell

Try this banishing spell to send unwanted energies and enemies packing. This unwanted enemy could be a specific person who is threatening or hurtful to you, an oppressive system that you are wanting to weaken and unravel, or any other sort of negative influence or energy you wish to be rid of. Please remember that if you ever feel your physical safety is threatened, report it to law enforcement immediately; you can cast spells after more mundane measures have been employed. Whomever or whatever the "enemy" may be, write this name on a small scrap of black cloth. Use a natural material such as cotton or hemp, or substitute with a small strip of paper. Use black ink to write the name. Burn this outside during a waning moon, holding the fabric or paper with tongs and placing it in the flame of a black candle set upon a fireproof dish. As you do so, imagine the moon as a deep hole, an open space, the waiting mouth of a bubbling cauldron. Envision the moon taking in the enemy, the enemy absorbed into darkness, into shadow, just as the moon's light wanes and disappears each lunar cycle. If you like, add this verse:

(Name of thing to be banished), I send your darkness
back into the night with the waning moon!
No longer can you harm!
No longer can you hurt!
You are weak! You are nowhere!
You are expelled from this space!
There is nowhere to go except back to your home!
Back into the darkness!
Back into the night!
Back into the moon
in her dying light!
You can no longer fight!

> To my will, you will bend!
> Your light may shine on,
> but your darkness now ends!

Burn the fabric or paper completely, then dump the ashes into the dirt and stomp on them to make sure that everything is fully extinguished and sufficiently cooled. Walk away and don't look back at the spot. Shake off the spell's energy (think wet dog shaking off to dry), and wash your hands and face in cool water. Then do something to get your mind off the spell. If it enters your thoughts, just repeat to yourself, "You are banished! It is done." Try a change of scenery or company if you're finding it difficult to get your mind off the matter.

• • • SPELL 5 • • •

Waning Moon Spell to Conceal a Secret

If you have a secret you wish to keep concealed, try this charm. On a waning crescent moon or at the dark moon, find a willow tree—preferably growing near water—and place your hand upon it. Say:

> Willow wood, I ask of you,
> please keep my secret!
> Keep it true!

Willow tree, I ask of thee,

please hold my secret!

Hold it deep!

Within your wood like lock and key,

these words are tied!

Remain unseen!

(repeat last stanza three times)

Place your lips gently against the trunk of the tree and whisper your secret.

• • • SPELL 6 • • •
Waning Moon Spell for Healing Emotional Wounds

This spell can help you kickstart the process of working through emotional wounds that are having a negative impact on your life. Don't begin this spellwork until you're ready to commit to what could very well be a long and painful healing process. The thing about ridding ourselves of past emo-

The moon rotates on its axis just as the earth does, but since the moon's rotation is roughly synchronized with the spin of the earth, we only ever see one side of it.

tional pains is that doing so reveals all the dark stuff we have buried even deeper. Each layer peeled away reveals another. It's kind of like when you start spring cleaning your house, and the more you get done, the more you realize all the hidden spots of dust and grime that have hitherto been overlooked. The deeper you get into your healing process, the harder it becomes. But this hardship is only temporary, and by processing through as much of the negative stuff as you can, you make room for more light and goodness and love to enter into your life. This spell can give you the extra support and transformative power needed to go through the process and emerge in a place of healing and inner peace that, in turn, invites you to make significant and lasting positive changes in your life and in your mindset.

You will need a cup, a candle, and a pitcher of clear, cool drinking water. During a waning moon, go outside and place your palms against the earth. If you're unable to get down to touch the earth, you can hold a rock to the same effect and simply cast the rock back into nature once you are done. Think of the healing, nourishing qualities of the moon, and say this verse:

I ask of you, moon, to heal me and hold me!

Soothe me and mold me!

My mother, don't forsake me!

I need you now to hold me!

Now with your hands on the earth, allow the painful feelings you wish to be rid of to flow out of you through your palms, into the neutralizing earth mingled with the moon's healing power. Think about the false beliefs you may have acquired as a result of abusive people, abusive words, abusive actions. Are there beliefs you hold about yourself that are limiting? Do you treat yourself with cruelty that is unjust and undeserved? Look head-on at all this bad stuff and call it out, literally commanding it to leave your body and ordering it to go out through your hands and into the earth. This process isn't pleasant—expect to get emotional. Let yourself take a break when you need to, or step away completely and try again when you are more ready if it becomes overwhelming in the moment. Once you feel you have expelled into the earth as much of these unpleasant emotions as you possibly can at the moment, take your hands off the ground. Shake them off and rub them together to remove any lingering negative energy. Think of your need and desire for renewal while you fill the cup with water from the pitcher, and think of your ability to rejuvenate just like the earth and moon. Pour this water out over the spot of ground where you placed your hands previously and envision the water washing away and transforming all the unwanted suffering so that what is new and wanted can grow in its place. Rinse out the cup with another splash of water, then fill it again. Hold the cup in your hands and think about what you wish to invite into your inner space. What do you welcome into the sacred space that is you? With what do you wish to fill your cup? Imagine these desired energies filling your cup. Drink the contents, sprinkling the last few droplets upon the ground. You may want to repeat this ritual several times during the waning moon, culminating on the nights of the dark moon before the moon once again becomes visible.

• • • SPELL 7 • • •
Dark Moon Binding Spell

Cast this binding spell at the time of the dark moon to get rid of anything unwanted in your life. Hold a length of black string in your hands, and think of the thing you wish to bind, be it a bad habit, baneful gossip, or something more sinister. Think of the essence of the thing to be bound, speak its name, and cast these thoughts into the string. Set the string to the side for a moment. Now think of the energy and pull of the dark moon, and call this power into your hands. Pick up the string again, and wrap it tightly and repeatedly around an iron nail, tying the string into many knots along the way. As you tie the knots, envision the thing to be bound imploding in on itself, becoming smaller and weaker, diminished and defeated, bound and restrained. After the nail is prepared, bury it deep in the ground then grind your foot over the spot as you speak this verse:

I bind you up in the shadows of the moon!
I tie you down in your darkness and spite!

Bound in the darkness!
Ended and over!
Into the shadows,
and out of my sight!

May the dark moon's shadow devour thee,
and lock you up, and eat the key!
(repeat the final stanza three times)

Dark Moon Devotion

Try this dark moon devotion to help you connect with the energies of the dark moon and utilize those energies to propel you forward in your magical craft. If you don't have a dark and quiet place outdoors to practice, you can do this inside in a darkened room. Place a black candle before you, but don't light it yet. Sit in the darkness and attune with the energies of the night. Close your eyes after a while to make the darkness complete. Notice what you feel. What thoughts or feelings crop up? Are you having any uncomfortable emotions? Examine closely any unpleasant sensations, and try to pinpoint the belief behind the feeling. Try to evaluate objectively whether or not that belief is accurate or logical. You may find that some of your fears are easily dispersed upon further inspection! Can you experience the darkness as a place of safety, like a protective womb that nourishes and shields you, or like the dark earth enveloping a small seed until it's ready to burst into life? Make peace with the feelings you find in the darkness. When you're ready, open your eyes and light the candle. Notice the thoughts or images that pop into your head upon that first spark of light. Notice any changes in your inner sensations. What are you feeling now? Gaze at the candle flame while you think about the dark moon reemerging into a thin crescent of silvery light. Do you have a "light" within you that is also ready to reemerge? Is there an area of spiritual or magical growth you would like to focus on, or are there specific goals you would like to achieve? Take a moment to set these intentions. You can incorporate these words if you like:

Great moon, as you come back

into my sight,

Great moon, as you come back

in growing light,

Let my light too, emerge anew!

Let my light too, grow bright and true!

As I so will it, so I am!

As the great moon wills it, so I can!

Extinguish the candle. If the idea is appealing to you, follow by making a list of steps you can take toward achieving your goals.

• • •

Chapter Six

SPECIAL MOON
MAGIC

There are a number of special lunar conditions that may occur throughout the year that offer their own unique opportunities for moon magic. These "special moons" include partial and total lunar eclipses, blue moons, blood moons, and supermoons. In this chapter, you'll find astronomical descriptions of these atypical lunar occurrences, along with some ideas for making magic on these special nights. You can perform a search on the internet or consult an astronomical or astrological guide to quickly find the dates of any upcoming super-moons, eclipses, and other lunar oddities.

Supermoon

A supermoon occurs when either a full moon or new moon coincides with the moon reaching its point of perigee, the place in its elliptical orbit where it makes its closest approach to the earth. On a full supermoon, the moon can appear around 14 percent larger than its average size, and the light from the sun that it reflects back to earth can shine up to 30 percent brighter. Observing the effect around sunset as the full moon begins to rise seems to enhance the moon's size even more, as objects seen close to the horizon appear larger to our eyes. There may be several supermoons in a single year, so search on the internet for "supermoons" followed by the year for which you're seeking information, and you'll find all the dates on which they will occur.

• • • SPELL 8 • • •
Supermoon Spell for Magnified Magic

You can take advantage of the magnified lunar energies that come with a supermoon to magnify the power of your magic. It's an especially advantageous time to boost magical power and increase psychic skill, and it's also an ideal time to charge magical tools and supplies such as crystals and candles to be used in lunar magic. If you have a new tarot deck sitting around that you haven't gotten around to charging yet, this might be a good time to finally bust it out and empower it with the benefit of the increased light of the moon.

Arrange thirteen clear quartz crystals in a circle under the light of a rising full supermoon. Place whatever you wish to charge with the magnified lunar energies in the middle of the ring of crystals. If it is yourself whom you wish to empower with greater ability and energy, stand in the middle of the circle. Face the moon as it rises over the horizon, and open yourself and any objects to be charged to the flow of this tremendous power. Give the increased luminosity space to freely flow and shine within you and upon you, or within and upon the objects you are charging. You can use this verse to help you call upon and imbue the lunar energy:

I welcome in the power of the moon!

Let a drop of your light reside here!

Lend me a cup of your force to imbibe here!

Let nature's will come ride here!

I welcome in the power of the moon!

Stay under the moonlight for a while or leave any objects to be charged outside to soak up as much lunar energy as possible. Be sure to retrieve your items before moonset.

• • •

Blue Moon

The term "blue moon" is commonly used to describe the second of two full moons that happen to fall within a given month, or the third of four full moons that occur within the same season. There is also the astrological blue moon, which describes the second full moon to occur consecutively in the same zodiac sign. We associate blue moons with the rare, the unexpected, and the nearly impossible made possible. We associate blue moons with oddities and mysticism, with peculiarities and magical experiences. The common expression "once in a blue moon" reveals the belief that this uncommon occurrence can lead to unlikely happenings and unexpected events. It's a time of mystery, and a time when those last shreds of hope can be woven into new cords that reaffirm possibility and activate new potentials.

Blue Moon Spell for New Possibility

If you have some magic to accomplish that you feel is nearly impossible, or if you are hoping on a long shot, try this blue moon spell to help transform the unlikely into a very real possibility.

Think of the long shot or improbability you are hoping for, and write on a piece of paper (or type and print) a past-tense account of this event as if it has already occurred. For example, if I was hoping to get a job in management with an organization called the Superhero Justice Alliance, I might write a headline that proclaims, "Melanie Marquis Named New Head of Superhero Justice Alliance," followed by an account of how I gave a stellar interview and about how my skills are already helping me succeed. Elaborate however you like, writing in the past tense as if this has already occurred and keeping it positive and optimistic in tone. Take this paper outside under a blue moon and read it all the

Pointing at the moon is said to bring bad luck.

way through out loud or to yourself. Then lay the paper down flat, place your palm and fingers upon it, and say:

> This is now possible.
>
> I open the way!
>
> I invite this reality to come through the gate!
>
> Once in a blue moon!
>
> Once in a true moon!
>
> Grant me this wish soon!
>
> Make this come true soon!

Fold the paper into thirds and draw on the outside of the paper a circle to symbolize the full moon. Color the circle in with a bright blue colored pencil or marker. Carry this paper with you or keep it on your altar or in another special place until your improbability proves itself possible by occurring.

• • •

Blood Moon

The term "blood moon" can cause some confusion, as it's used in several different ways. The moon during any total lunar eclipse may be called a blood moon, as the moon inevitably takes on a reddish color as the earth's shadow falls upon its surface. The term is also used in a more specific sense to describe a lunar tetrad, a series of four total lunar eclipses in a row, each occurring six lunar months apart. The name "Blood Moon" also sometimes refers to the first full moon following the full moon nearest the Autumn Equinox, which is also sometimes called the Hunter's Moon. Rising large above the horizon as the sun sets and lingering low in the sky, the full moon during autumn can frequently appear to have an orangish, almost reddish hue. "Blood moon" can be used to describe the color of the moon anytime it takes on a red-orange glow. Being the color of blood, red is often associated with health, strength, vitality, and energy, but a reddish moon might also be perceived as an ominous sign that brings to mind the spilled blood of warfare and death. When the moon takes on a reddish tone, it's a good time to do defensive magic and strengthening spells to help fortify your protections and increase your vital force.

• • • SPELL 10 • • •
Blood Moon Spell for Defense and Vitality

To renew your personal defenses and amplify your vitality, here's a spell to try when the moon looks red. Recline or lay down outside and place a bloodstone on your chest and place a moonstone on your forehead. Feel the energies of

MOONCAKES

In China, the Mid-Autumn Festival is held each year on the fifteenth day of the eighth lunar month in honor of the moon goddess Chang'O. One special tradition celebrated at this time is the eating of mooncakes, thick round pastries that are filled with bean paste or lotus seed paste. Friends and family gather outside beneath a full moon to share mooncakes and express gratitude for their blessings. Eating a mooncake at the Mid-Autumn Festival is believed to invite good fortune and prosperity.

the moon flowing through the rocks and into your body. Feel the energy flow from the bottoms of your feet up through the top of your head. Imagine the energy moving freely along this path, spiraling upwards uninhibited, casting aside any obstacles that stand in the way of the unstoppable current of power that is coursing through your being. Imagine yourself as all-powerful, having the strength of the universe, the might of the galaxies at your command. Let this power flow through you as the stones align your vibrations to their energies. Open your mind to wisdom and healing, and open your heart to courage and strength. When you're through, tie the stones up in a red cloth and keep it close to your body for health and protection.

• • •

Lunar Eclipse

Lunar eclipses occur when the earth is in perfect or near-perfect alignment with the moon and sun, causing earth's shadow to fall upon the face of the moon. Since ancient times, many people have met a lunar eclipse with caution and a great cacophony of sound or with other powerfully protective rituals. The lunar eclipse is the only time that we see the shadow of our own planet, literally and symbolically bringing us face to face with our individual and collective "dark side." Lunar eclipses are good opportunities for moon magic intended to banish, bind, or transform.

Lunar Eclipse Banishing Ritual

Try this ritual during a lunar eclipse to banish the shadows in your life that block the light. You'll need something to make a good bit of noise. You might choose a drum, a set of cymbals, or some pots and pans to bang on. If you need to maintain a relative quiet, a rattle or a bell could work to the same effect. You might choose to use your own body as the noisemaker, stomping your feet, clapping your hands, or howling and yelling. Sit quietly as you wait for the eclipse to begin. Once it starts, let the feeling of the moment envelop you. Do you feel a sense of stillness about the world, or does it seem more like a sense of uneasiness? Do you feel any shadows upon the earth that are ready to be lifted away? Do you feel any shadows within yourself that you are ready to expel completely? Begin making noise with your noisemakers of choice, thinking as you do so of these shadows being chased away by the soundwaves you have sent reverberating through the air. As you exhale, push any unwanted feelings outside of yourself. Let any negative emotions of guilt, restriction, or regret glide away from you, opening up within you an expansive space that is free and sacred. As the mood strikes you, continue making noise periodically until the moon begins to return and you feel as though the shadows have been thoroughly chased away. You might use the time when the light of the moon is returning to celebrate this lunar victory, making sounds of celebration, dancing, or clapping to help raise the energy of the moon's return. Take a shower when you are done to finish cleansing yourself of any lingering unwanted vibrations.

• • • SPELL 12 • • •
Lunar Eclipse Binding Spell

Use this spell to bind and diminish unwanted influences and obstacles that you feel are hindering your way forward. Take a piece of obsidian and hold it in your hand as you think of that which you wish to be rid of. Imagine that the stone in your hand is filling with the energies of the thing to be banished or bound, taking in all this power and weaving it into its inner matrix. Envision the surface of the stone now closing off, sealing out anything from getting in, and more importantly, sealing in what is now inside it. Bury the stone once the moon is notably obscured in the shadow of earth. As you spread the dirt over the spot and pat it down firmly, you can use these words to help seal the spell:

What is born from the dark, goes back to the dark!

There is no other path than the path I set.

There is no other course! There is no recourse!

Go back underground or let the moon take you yet!

• • • SPELL 13 • • •

Lunar Eclipse Ritual for Transformation

This lunar eclipse ritual is very adaptable, in that you can use it to diminish or destroy, and increase or attract, just about anything. Don't feel confined to the example given here; use it as a guide to design your own ritual that's precisely fitted to your purpose.

You'll need paper, scissors, something round you can trace (such as a drinking glass), a black marker, and a red marker. Trace two circles, one with the black marker and one with the red marker. Cut them out. On the circle you traced with the black marker, use the same marker to write the name of the thing you wish to diminish, or create a symbol of it. For example, if you are wanting to reduce feelings of insecurity, you might write the word "insecurity" on the circle, or you might instead choose to draw a symbol that represents these feelings, such as a heart inside a cage. Decorate the circle however you like so that you can envision it as a solid representation of whatever it is you are wishing to be rid of.

Next, turn your attentions to the circle you traced with the red marker. Think of what you wish to increase or attract, that which will take the place of the thing that is to be diminished. Use the red marker to decorate the circle with words or symbols to represent whatever it is you are wishing to welcome in greater abundance. Using our example above of "insecurity," you might mark the other circle with symbols and words to represent confidence and courage, ability and empowerment.

Now hold each completed circle in turn, one at a time starting with the circle drawn in black, as you let the feelings and energies of what that circle represents flow through you and out of you and into the circle you hold in your hands. When it is time for the lunar eclipse, set the circle traced in red to the side and place the circle traced in black before you, along with the black marker. Put the circle on top of a notepad or sturdy piece of paper. As the earth's shadow begins to obscure the moon, start scribbling over the interior of the circle, coloring it in to mimic the shaded part of the moon. Do just a little at a time, corresponding with the growing shadow upon the face of the moon. As more of the moon becomes obscured, color in more of the circle to match. Color with intention and ferocity. Feel your power and let this power flow through you and out of the marker. You might imagine your markings as an intensifying and expanding shadow that is plunging into darkness and obscurity all that the circle represents. You might imagine a majestic dragon that is devouring its prey. If it's a partial eclipse, when the moon reaches its greatest obscurity, go ahead and color in the remainder of the circle.

Now pick up the circle decorated in red representing what you wish to welcome and increase, and slide it underneath the now completely black circle so that the black circle is on top of it, perfectly aligned. As the moon's light begins to return, start slowly sliding the black circle off the other circle, so that this underlying circle becomes more and more visible to correspond with the moon's growing light. Just as you colored in the black circle in stages, do this in stages as well, periodically sliding the black circle just ever so slightly in sync with the moon's return. When the moon has come back fully into view and your circle of what you wish to welcome is fully visible, crumple up the black circle and either burn it to ashes or toss it over your left shoulder for now and put it in the recycling bin after your ritual is complete.

Return your attentions to the remaining paper circle, and feel the vibrations of what this circle represents flow into you and through you. Feel the moonlight streaming down into the circle, magnifying these energies that will soon be manifest in your life. Take some time to imagine in detail and with the corresponding emotions what it will be like to have your wish fulfilled. When you are finished, keep the circle someplace safe but where it is uncovered. Touch it daily as you consciously reaffirm your intention for increasing or manifesting whatever the circle represents to you.

• • •

Chapter Seven

MOON SPELLS BY GOAL

In this chapter, you'll find a selection of moon spells arranged alphabetically by the goal or intention of the magic. While some of these spells suggest a specific lunar phase in which to cast the magic, most of the spells provided in this chapter can be performed anytime. Adjust and adapt these spells to suit your needs and personal practices.

Abundance Spell

Use this recipe and ritual to invite a greater flow of abundance into your life. If possible, share this ritual with family or friends. Pour one cup of jasmine rice into a pot. Use a silver spoon to gently push the rice into the shape of a waxing crescent moon, its horns pointing to your left as you gaze into the pot. Hold your hand above the rice as you think of the thing you wish to welcome in greater abundance, be it love, joy, money, friendships, or a bountiful vegetable harvest. Imagine the energy of your thoughts flowing into the rice. Now pour two cups of water into a separate container and invite the energies of the moon to enter into the water. You can take it outside and hold it up to the sky or place it near a window facing the direction of the moon. Think of the moonlight streaming into the water, charging it with an immense power and pull of attraction. Think of the moon's glow increasing; think of how it appears to expand each month from a crescent into a full circle, and send these thoughts into the water. Now pour this water into the pot and over the rice as you envision the abundance you desire. Feel an emotion of gratitude and optimism in your heart as you see yourself immersed in an abundant flow of whatever it is you are seeking. See yourself embracing this abundance, and do your best to conjure the feelings of knowing you deserve this abundance. Bring the water and rice to a boil for about a minute, then turn the heat down to a simmer and cover the pot. Let it cook for about 15 to 20 minutes until the water is absorbed, then turn off the heat. Notice how much the rice has expanded in the pot. Fluff the rice with a fork as you think again of the thing you want in abundance, imagining that you are expanding and increasing this just as you are expanding the volume of the rice. After fluffing the rice, pour it out onto a large plate or cutting board, and use a silver spoon to gently shape the rice into a circular mound. If possible, take the rice outside to eat it under the moonlight. If that's not possible, you might light a silver candle or set out a crystal or moonstone in honor of the moon as you eat the rice indoors. Share the rice if you can. If that's not possible, you might want to reduce the recipe to one fourth of the above proportions so you're able to eat the entire amount yourself.

Banishing Spell

Find a twig or small stick that has an outer layer of bark on it. Use a pencil to inscribe along the side of the stick a name or symbol to represent the negative energy or obstacle you are hoping to banish or overcome. You'll also need a piece of coarse or medium-grit sandpaper. Cut the sandpaper into the shape of a crescent moon. You can work this spell over the course of several nights while the moon is waning, or you can complete it all at once, syncing the climax of your spell to the time of moonset. When you're ready, go outside with the stick and the sandpaper. Set the sandpaper down before you and place upon it a piece of selenite. Hold the stick in your hands and think about it as if you are holding the obstacle or negativity that you wish to banish. Think of it in your mind as more than a symbol—pretend it is the actual energy and essence of whatever it is you're aiming to remove from your life. Now place the stick before you and pick up the selenite. Hold the selenite in your hands and think about its changing nature, its ephemeral qualities. A slight tilt of the stone and the light reflecting off its surface changes; a slight scratch or impact, and a layer is set loose from the whole. Rest the selenite on your lap if you're sitting down, or place it near you. Pick up the sandpaper and the stick. As you think of the moon making its arc across the sky or the waning moon's diminishing light, rub the sandpaper against the stick, removing the inscription, removing the bark particle by particle. Imagine that as you do so, the obstacle represented by that stick is also stripped away, worn down, and diminished into oblivion. Link this action to the action of the moon: think about how the moon is setting or its size is reducing, just as you sand away at the stick, just as you are wearing down your obstacles. Once the stick is completely sanded, leave it outside near a tree with the thought in mind that it can now become something new, perhaps a part of a bird's nest, or perhaps a child's magic wand.

The craters on the moon were formed by asteroids and other space debris pounding into the lunar surface.

• • • SPELL 16 • • •
Beauty Spell

Use this spell to help increase your inner and outer beauty. While we all have the potential to be beautiful, it's also a fact that next to being mean-spirited, nothing makes a person uglier than a lack of confidence. In other words, when we act ugly or we feel ugly, we actually do appear less attractive than we could be. Feeling beautiful and acting beautiful, on the other hand, can greatly enhance our appeal and improve the aesthetics of our image. Everyone has what are perceived as "flaws," and it's difficult to avoid focusing on the flaws that we ourselves possess. If you think about it objectively, however, you may realize that you tend to be far more critical and judgmental of yourself than you are of others. There's never a reason to be more cruel to yourself than you are to other people, so challenge any negative self-talk regarding what you see as your flaws. As a mental exercise, imagine someone you think of as super beautiful, and then imagine that person having the same so-called "flaws" you believe you have. Does the person become any less attractive to you? Is this person's true beauty actually affected in any way, or do you still find them just as appealing as you did before you imagined them with the "flaw"? Chances are, your image of the person won't be much diminished by the addition of a few stretch marks, some extra curves, some loose skin, a few wrinkles, a raging pimple, or whatever else it might be. We overlook the outward "flaws" of others because inner beauty not only outweighs, but also actually produces, outward beauty. Try this spell to help realize your already existent beauty and to magnify and increase your attractiveness and appeal to others. Charge a piece of selenite with the light of a waxing or full moon, or whenever the moon can be seen close to venus in the sky. Hold the selenite in your hand as you think about a thread of energy connecting the moon to the stone. Envision the lunar rays pouring into the selenite. Rub the selenite gently over your face and body, envisioning the cells of your body rejuvenating and transforming inside and out with a renewed vitality wherever the stone is touching. Envision the moonlight pouring down on you and flowing over you like a shower, cleansing and invigorating your entire body. Imagine yourself as the most beautiful and glowing version of yourself imaginable. If you like, use these words to strengthen the charm:

Lady Luna, bright and true!

Make me shine as bright as you!

Place a moonbeam in my eyes,

and pour your shimmer on my skin.

True beauty, like the moon, will rise!

Rejuvenating what's within!

Hang the selenite by your mirror or place it on your dressing table or another area of your home associated with personal appearance and grooming.

Charm Spell

Use this moon spell to enhance your charm, beauty, and charisma whenever you wish to shine with the enchanting magnetism of the magnificent moon. Take a chalice of water outside and lift it up toward the moon as if you are making a toast. Envision the moonlight streaming through the sky and into your cup. Think of the beauty of the moonlight; conjure up your most genuine feelings of adoration and admiration for the glorious moon. Whether it's the crescent moon's silvery smile that pleases you, or whether it's the way a full moon can light up the night making more mischief possible that you adore, reflect honestly on what you think is beautiful and enchanting about the moon, and let the feelings behind those thoughts swell in your heart. Let these emotions extend beyond you, into the sky and to the moon. Welcome the moon's energy to flow back into you, first exhaling deeply to clear your inner space, then inhaling with equal fervor as you draw those lunar energies into your body. Keep breathing in the moon until you feel full of this energy, letting it emanate from your physical body to fill also the space encompassed by your energetic aura. Drink deeply from the cup. Imagine yourself glowing with moonlight, then imagine this moonlight integrating itself into the clothing or jewelry you're wearing. Give the moon your thanks, and pour the remaining water on the ground as an offering. Proceed into the night with confidence, knowing that the moon's glowing aura surrounds you, giving you the power to charm anyone with whom you interact.

• • • SPELL 18 • • •
Clarity Spell

If you're feeling muddled or you're having trouble making a decision, try this moon spell for clarity. Add a pinch of sea salt to a glass of drinking water and take it outside under the moonlight. Imagine the glass of water as a cup containing the wisdom and essence of the oceans. Think about the moon's gravitational pull on the ocean's waters as you take a small sip. Now take a translucent piece of aquamarine and dip it into the water. Now look through the wet stone at the moonlight. You can use this verse if you like to help express your intention for insight:

Wisdom of the oceans,

Power of the moon!

Wisdom of the stone and earth,

Power of the moon!

Knowing moon! Bright moon! Wise moon!

Show me what I need to know,

Show it to me soon!

Think about your quandary; as you contemplate different possibilities and hunches, notice how the quality of the light shining through the stone transforms. Does the light become dimmer or brighter? Does it shift? Does it disappear entirely? How do your gut feelings change as your thoughts flow? If you need additional insight, pour the rest of the water around you in a circle and keep the aquamarine close by as you consult the tarot or another divination device for further details.

• • • SPELL 19 • • •
Dream Spell

Use this charm to help encourage prophetic dreaming, or to help facilitate lucid dreaming or other types of dream work. Take a fresh leaf of mugwort and wrap it around a piece of serpentine. Tie the bundle up with a black string. If you don't have fresh mugwort, you can use the dried leaves instead, and use a small circle of black or purple fabric to hold everything in place. Using your fingertip or wand tip dipped in coconut oil, water, or an appropriate lunar potion, trace a symbol of the moon on the fresh leaf or on the outside of the fabric that's wrapped around the dried herbs. Place this outside for a while under the light of the moon if possible. Alternatively, you might place it on top of the Moon tarot card and leave it resting on your altar for a bit, or place it on top of a photograph or other image of the moon. Before you go to sleep, hold the bundle in your hands and think of what you are hoping to dream about. If you have a question you want answered, state that question clearly in your mind and think of your intention to wake up with further insight. Place the bundle beneath your pillow, and put a notebook and pen near your bed. When you awaken, write down anything you can remember from your dreams, even if all you have are vague impressions or sensations. Don't worry about analyzing anything until you've recollected as much as you can. Later in the day once you're fully awake, take some time to look at what you wrote down and see if there is any more you can remember. If you don't have success on the first try, don't be discouraged. Repeat the method regularly, and soon you will train your mind to the process. When you're ready to create a fresh dream charm, you can sew the old mugwort into a small pillow or incorporate it into a sachet to hang near your bed to further facilitate your dreamwork. Just be sure the bundle isn't accessible to small children or pets, as mugwort can be toxic to some animals and may cause allergic reactions in people with certain allergies.

• • • SPELL 20 • • •
Employment Spell

Try this spell if you are hoping to get a new job or advance your career. Write your full name on a piece of paper and surround this with seven pieces of star anise. Sprinkle some vanilla powder or oil over your name. Draw a circle repeatedly around your name and the star anise as you envision with each circle that you are drawing down lunar energies into the paper, focusing on your name like a spotlight. As you do so, repeat your full name in your mind and state that you are the best person for the job. For instance, if I was casting this spell, my thoughts would be "Melanie Marquis is the best person for the job" or "Melanie Marquis is the right choice!" If I happen to know who is in charge of making the decisions, I would envision that person thinking those words as they hold my résumé or application or consider me for a promotion. As you say the words and circle your name, imagine yourself performing the job in question and excelling at it. See yourself carrying out your job duties and imagine yourself interacting with co-workers. Imagine receiving your first big paycheck and depositing this money into the bank. Wrap the star anise in the paper, and place it all in a gold, green, or silver cloth. Tie it with a red ribbon. Take this little bundle with you on all job interviews, and place it for a while on top of any applications or resumes you plan to send. Before you step into any place of potential employment, squeeze the bundle and repeat to yourself that you are the best person for the job and that you are the right choice.

• • • SPELL 21 • • •
Fertility Spell

Use this spell to help encourage fertility in plants or people. Fertility is a concept that encompasses more than reproduction of the species. It is the energy of active creation, the energy of prolific production, in which we may all take part. This spell can be useful not only for those who want to encourage physical fertility, but also for artists, writers, and other creative types who are experiencing a block in the usual flow of inspiration or productivity.

Begin by choosing an image of a rabbit. It can be a photograph, a painting, a figurine, or a stuffed animal. If the spell is intended to encourage your own fertility, place the image of the rabbit on your altar or in another special place in your home. If it's intended to increase the fertility of plants, place the image of the rabbit in the area where the plants are growing. Use a lip liner pencil in a shade of red or pink to draw a crescent moon shape on the belly of the rabbit, the horns of the moon pointing upwards. Think of the fertility you wish for as you draw the symbol, and think of that crescent moon shape as a belly or womb that will nourish those areas where you wish to encourage prolific growth. If you prefer, you can use a permanent marker, plain water, a lunar potion, olive oil, or coconut oil to make the symbol. If you've chosen a stuffed animal for your rabbit symbol, just stick with the plain water, or draw a symbol on a piece of fabric and tie it onto the stuffed animal like a bib or scarf. Hold your hands lov-

> Cutting your hair when the moon is waxing is believed to increase hair growth.

ingly on or near your rabbit symbol as you envision the fertility you are seeking. Imagine the moonlight pouring down like nourishing rain upon the seeds you wish to grow. You can use this verse to petition the moon for assistance and to aid in your visualization if needed:

Rabbit of the moon!

I open this space to new life in abundance!

May your life-giving elixir rain down upon this fertile ground!

I will nourish this seed with love and with light!

Rabbit of the moon!

Help this sacred seed to grow!

Rabbit of the moon!

Please bless me with your magic!

Hop through the field and let it grow in abundance!

Hop through the field and bring new life!

Rabbit of the moon, I ask you!

Please hop through the field and bring new life!

Place an offering in front of the rabbit. You might offer some smooth, shiny round stones, some flowers, some herbs such as rosemary and vanilla, some oils such as olive or coconut oil, or a pomegranate. Keep the rabbit in its station, and place new offerings as you feel inclined. Be sure to express gratitude when your wish is fulfilled.

• • • SPELL 22 • • •
Growth Spell

Cast this spell for growth and expansion during a waxing moon. To begin, you'll need to make a crescent-shaped moon out of dough or clay to represent that which you wish to grow and expand. You can make your own special clay or dough to use in this spell, or you can purchase ready-made play dough or clay and use that instead. If you're going to make your own dough or clay blend, there are many recipes online or you can get creative. Two cups of flour mixed with one cup of salt, two cups of water, and several tablespoons of vegetable oil provides a good base dough, or if you have soil that is rich in clay in your area, you can scoop some up and mix it with water until it's a good consistency. If you live in a place with more sandy soil, you might choose to go for an adobe mixture, blending the dirt with water and hay or another dried plant fiber such as hemp. You might choose to mix additional herbs and oils in with your clay or dough to help imitate your intention. For instance, if your desire is to grow your network of friends, you might mix some rosemary in with your dough, as this herb has strong associations with friendship and affection. If you're wanting to grow your wealth, you might mix a few coins into the dough.

Think of whatever it is that you are wanting to grow as you work with your clay, shaping it into a crescent moon shape. Place your creation on a plate or tray, and take it outside or put it on your lunar altar. Hold your hands above the clay as you envision the growing appearance of the waxing moon, seeing in a moment in your mind's eye a sped-up version of the moon's transformation. As you imagine the moon growing larger, culminating in a full moon, gently press the dough so that it expands in size, just as the moon will appear to do as it further waxes. Think also of that which is represented in the clay, growing right alongside the moon. Link these energies in your mind and think of them both expanding and growing together in unison. You can leave your clay creation outdoors and leave it at that, or you can let it air dry or bake it if you wish to keep it as a talisman. The basic play dough recipe given above can be baked in the oven at a low heat of around 215–275 degrees F for anywhere from 12 to 45 minutes, depending on the size and thickness of your creation. Check it frequently (every few minutes), and take it out when it starts to feel mostly hardened. The dough may harden a little further as it cools. You can keep this magical moon as a talisman that will impart the expansive essence of the waxing moon to whatever it is you wish to grow.

• • • SPELL 23 • • •
Healing Spell

Try this spell to open yourself to healing energies. If possible, go outside where you can see the moon. If that's not possible, you can simply imagine the moon orbiting around the earth, traveling with us as we circle the sun. Now envision your body as housing within it a sacred space—your own space. Are you getting uncomfortable feelings from this space? Is there anything lingering here that you would rather not welcome in this space anymore? Imagine as you exhale slowly and deeply that you are pushing out of your inner space anything that you do not welcome there. Once you feel that your inner space is as open and clear as you can possibly get it at this time, think of the healing energy that you welcome, an energy of love and will everlasting, a force of vitality, renewal, rejuvenation. Envision this energy amidst the many rays of moonlight reflecting down upon the earth and you.

MOONSTONE

Moonstone has been appreciated since ancient times for both its beauty and its magical attributes. The stone is said to have many mystical properties, including the ability to attract love and enhance psychic abilities. Some lore states that moonstone grows brighter during a full moon or when intuition is strong, while the stone is perceived to dim and lose its luster during a waning moon or when danger approaches. Especially lucky for travelers, lovers, fortunetellers, and witches, wear a moonstone to bring good luck to all your endeavors.

Invite into your body this healing power; imagine it as a soft, cool, purifying light streaming down from the moon into your body. Feel your love for the part of Nature that is you. Let the feeling of love and healing that you know deep down you deserve, to flow out from your heart and shine, wrapping around you in a soothing blanket of mercy and compassion. You can add this verse if you like, or express in another way that you welcome the moon's healing energies into the sacred space that is you:

> I welcome into me energies of healing!
>
> I welcome into me revitalizing light!
>
> I welcome into me powers of renewal!
>
> I welcome into me the moon's returning light!
>
> The moon renews and so will I!
>
> Shine like the full moon, whole and bright!
>
> (Repeat the final couplet three times,
>
> increasing the speed and emphasis of each repetition.)

• • • SPELL 24 • • •
Insight Spell

Use this spell to gain insight through your dreams. Write down on a piece of paper the insight you would like for your dreams to reveal, and place this under the moonlight surrounded by a circle of nine willow leaves. Think of the moonlight streaming down into the paper and willow, reading your intentions and magnifying the power of your will. Now tuck the nine willow leaves and the paper between your pillow and pillowcase. When you're ready to sleep, affirm in your mind that you are open and ready for insight. When you wake, don't start doing anything right away. Take a few moments to try to recollect as much as possible from your dreams and reflect on any feelings or insights you might have. Even when we don't remember the specific contents of our dreams, they often leave behind lingering emotions. We may also have previously forgotten images and scenes from our dreams pop back into our conscious awareness several hours or even days after waking from a powerful yet elusive dream, triggered by experiences or observations that connect to pieces of our dreams the subconscious mind has not forgotten.

• • • SPELL 25 • • •

Inspiration Spell

Use this spell whenever you feel like you're in a creative rut, or whenever you would welcome an extra boost of inspiration to fuel your imagination. Take some tools of your creative trade outdoors, or place them on or near your lunar altar, if it's feasible to do so. If you're a painter, for example, bring your paint brushes and palette. If you sew clothing designs, bring your needles and scissors. If you're a writer, bring your laptop or your notebook and a favorite pen. Take a few moments to focus your thoughts on the moon, then think about what you would like to achieve through your creative endeavors. What do you hope to bring to the world with the things you create? Think about all the goodness you can potentially bring through your creative art. Imagine the emotions that would accompany the achievement of creative success that benefits the world; feel these emotions in your heart and in your gut. Are you ready to achieve your maximum creative potential? If you feel in your heart that you are ready, express your desire and will to welcome new inspiration to take your work to greater heights. Imagine that you are literally pulling down the moonlight, grabbing it with your fingers and drawing it down through the sky and into your creative tools. Touch your tools as you imagine yourself succeeding in your craft, creating amazing works of your chosen art. Invite into yourself the power and light of the moon. You can end the spell with an expression of gratitude or an affirmation of readiness such as this:

Luna, guide me in my crafft!

Luna, sail within my heart!

Luna, flow into me now!

Luna, flow into my art!

Together, let's make magic!

Together, let's conspire!

Flow into me and through my art,

And millions, we'll inspire!

By the light of the moon!

By the deep of the sea!

As the moon and I will it,

Then so will it be!

(repeat final stanza 3 times.)

• • • SPELL 26 • • •
Love Spell

Use this spell to attract a suitable and enjoyable romantic partner to your life. You'll need three cherries with pits, some jasmine essential oil, vanilla oil, or olive oil, and a handful of fresh or dried basil leaves. You'll also need one piece of moonstone and aquamarine each, a circle of white fabric about six inches in diameter, and a piece of red, pink, blue, white, or silver ribbon.

Begin by letting your thoughts wander into romantic fantasies as you carefully eat the cherries one by one, taking care to set the pits aside as each one is revealed. Next, douse the cherry pits with jasmine, vanilla, or olive oil. Rub the oil all over the surface of each cherry pit, one by one. As you anoint the first cherry pit with the oil, think of yourself and the feeling of love you have to offer. Think of all the happiness and joy your love could bring to someone. As you anoint the second cherry pit, think of the feeling of love that you would like to receive from someone. Think of the way you want to feel around a person. What would their essence feel like? What sort of vibe would they have? Don't think too specifically in terms of appearance as this can limit the effect of the magic, but do try to imagine with as many details as possible the general energetic vibe or spiritual qualities with which you feel you can best connect. As you anoint the third cherry pit with the oil, imagine the feeling of being loved unconditionally and generously, and imagine yourself freely giving this same unconditional and generous love. Let those feelings and fantasies fill your heart as you rub this final cherry seed with the oil.

Sprinkle a handful of the basil leaves over the cherry pits, and roll them around in it until they're well covered. Place the circle of white fabric before you and think of this as representing the full moon. Put the cherry pits and an additional pinch of basil in the center of the fabric circle. Add to this a moonstone and a piece of aquamarine.

Invite the energy of the moon to lend itself to your magic. Envision your fabric moon drawing down the power and magnetism of the actual moon, filling the cherry pits, stones, and basil with an amplified vibration. Imagine the disparate energies coming together, combining and fusing into a synchronized pulse. Imagine this pulse streaming out from the ingredients before you like a homing signal, calling out into the night so that a person worthy of your heart will find you. Gather the fabric circle into a bundle and tie up the top with a red, pink, blue, white, or silver ribbon. Keep this bundle close to you until your wishes for love are fulfilled.

• • • SPELL 27 • • •
Luck Spell

When the moon can be observed in the sky passing near to Jupiter, the planet of luck, try this charm to help make a wish come true. You'll need a thirteen-inch length of shiny gray or silver thread, a three-inch length of yellow thread, a circle of purple fabric, vanilla essential oil or vanilla extract, and a dish of ground nutmeg. Begin by anointing the longer string with the vanilla, working from the middle outward toward both ends, then up and down the entire length of the thread. Think of your wish as you do so, allowing yourself to daydream and imagine as clearly as you can how you will feel and what it might be like when your wish is fulfilled. See the success you want, and feel the emotions of having achieved it. Now sprinkle some nutmeg on the string, and rub it in as you continue to imagine your wish being fulfilled. Now, shift your thinking so that your mind is focused on a concise expression of your wish. Repeat this wish thirteen times as you tie thirteen knots along the length of the string, beginning by tying a knot in the middle of the string, then tying six more knots above and six more knots below. Now coil the string into a small circle and place it in the dish of nutmeg. Cover the string completely with the powder.

Focus on the moon and Jupiter, and think of the energies of these celestial bodies flowing into the nutmeg-covered string. Imagine this as a circuitry through which energy is flowing back and forth. As the moon and Jupiter lend their energies into your magic, so too is the energetic impression of your wish sent back in reply. Now swirl your finger in three circles within the middle of the coiled string. State your wish clearly and with eager emphasis once more. Pour the nutmeg and the string onto the piece of purple fabric, gather it together, twist the top, and tie it up with the yellow string, making three knots. Draw on the bottom of the bindle the planetary symbol of Jupiter and an image of the moon in whatever phase it currently is in.

You can use these words to further magnify and seal the charm:

Zip, zap, into my trap!

What I seek falls onto my lap!

What I want, I'll get it now!

This wish so wills it!

Zip, zap, pow!

Lust Spell

Use this spell to magnify feelings of lust. You'll need two or more fresh, whole basil leaves, some jasmine essential oil, a length of purple string, and a white candle. Practice this spell at a waxing or full moon outdoors, or at your lunar altar. Light the white candle in honor of the moon as you feel in your heart your admiration and awe for the moon's indescribable beauty and immense power. Think of your intention to cast this spell with the moon as witness and ally. Anoint the basil leaves with the jasmine oil, touching each one in an affectionate way. Think of the leaves as representing yourself and any lovers or potential lovers you might desire. If you aren't intending for the spell to affect anyone but yourself, think of the two basil leaves as two aspects of yourself, the self you present to the world and the inner self that only you know. Or, you might think of the leaves as representing your reserved side and your wild side.

After you have lovingly anointed each leaf with the oil, gently rub the leaves together, imagining as you do so a feeling of lustful pleasure throughout your body. Now shape the purple string into a circle like a full moon, arranging it to form a ring around the candle. Invite the energies of the moon to enter into this thread. Focus your mind and heart on the essence of moonlight and lunar energy and imagine pulling this energy toward you and into the string. Now roll the leaves into a small scroll shape and use the purple thread to bind it. Start by tying the string around the bottom of the leaf scroll, then spiral it around toward the top and tie it off. As you bind the leaves together, you can add these words or simply focus your mind on your intentions:

Sealed with the moon and sealed with a kiss,

I open to a flow of bliss!

(repeat three times)

Kiss the leaf scroll to seal the spell. Extinguish the candle, then toss the leaf scroll into a natural body of moving water such as a river, or leave it amidst a patch of wild vegetation.

• • • SPELL 29 • • •
Magical Power Spell

Use this spell to help further open yourself to the natural forces and connecting threads that weave throughout the universe. Work this spell on the full moon if possible. Pick a space to do the spell, and in the north of the area, place a rock. In the east of the area, place some incense. Choose a scent that opens your senses and puts you in a mystical mood. In the south of the space, place a red or black candle. In the west of the space, place a bowl of water.

Begin by focusing your attention on your surrounding environment. Think of the earth beneath your feet giving you a solid foundation to stand on. Feel the air on your skin and feel it filling your lungs with each breath. Smell the vegetation surrounding you. Think of the other creatures that are sharing the space with you, the insects beneath the soil, the birds in the sky, the squirrels nestled high up in the treetops. Take notice of the moon and think of the moonlight washing over you, pouring down upon you like drops of rain. Think of the moonlight filling your being as if you are a vessel being filled with water. Sit with this energy; observe how this lunar light feels within your body.

Now turn your attentions to the elemental items you placed in each quadrant of your sacred space. Start at the north and place your hands on or above the rock. Open your hands to the energetic vibrations, and observe the sen-

The dark areas on the moon's surface are called the lunar maria, or lunar seas.

☆

sation of this energy. Now turn your attentions to the east and to the incense. Watch the smoke drift and swirl through the air. Breathe in the aroma and allow the scent to awaken your senses. As you exhale, think of the wind blowing through the tree branches, carrying seeds across the ground and through the air to a suitable place in which to take root. Let the energy of the air move through you. Think of your core as being an open window, and think of the air moving freely through you. Think of the energies comprising your body as a screen that is allowing this air to pass in and out uninhibited. Observe the sensation you get from the feel of air moving freely through your body, not just in and out of your lungs, but flowing through the entirety of your physical form as if you weren't quite solid.

Now focus on the candle in the south of your sacred space. Hold your hands close above the flame so that you can feel its warmth. Think of how relieving warmth is to a cold body. Think of the light of the sun that illuminates and warms our world by day, and guides us through the night as the moon shines back to us like a mirror the powerful rays of our home star just out of view. Rub your hands together briskly and feel the heat generated between your palms. Now hold your hands a few inches apart, palms facing, and think of the heat and light of a blazing fire. Call this heat into the space between your hands, as if you are holding it. Move your hands back and forth on this ball of energy and notice if it seems to grow hotter.

Now focus your attentions on the bowl of water in the western quadrant of your space. Gently glide your fingertips through the water and notice how it feels on your skin. Notice the ripples and motion of the water as you move it around with your fingers. Think of the fluidity of water, how it can adapt to the shape of any container you put it in, and how it can literally carve a landscape, forging canyons and ravines where once was solid stone.

Now focus your attentions back on the moon. Envision a thread of energy trailing down from the moon, into the top of your head, and straight down through your body and through the bottoms of your feet to connect to the earth below. From this centered feeling, see if you can connect to each of the elemental items you placed at the quadrants, this time while remaining in the middle of the space and without the benefit of getting physically close to the items. Think of the energies and essence of each element, and think about your desire to call forth these energies. Feel the energetic essence of the element and imagine that you are literally pulling this energy toward you from the earth, from the air, from the fire, from the water. Envision the energies of these elements streaming into you, each connecting to the thread of power that unites you with the moon.

Pick up the rock and hold it firmly in your hand. Dip it in the water. Then pass it through the candle flame, then waft it through the incense smoke. Now hold the rock up to the sky and invite the energies of the moon to come into the stone and enjoy a refuge and audience there. On one side of the rock, draw a lunar symbol such as the triple moon symbol featuring a full moon flanked by waxing and waning crescents. On the other side of the rock, write your full name and beneath this draw a lightning bolt. Keep this rock nearby during spellcasting to add power, or carry it close to your body to help you become more sensitive to nature's energies and help sharpen your ability to guide these energies through your magic.

• • • SPELL 30 • • •
Manifestation Spell

Work this spell all at once, or repeat it for up to seven consecutive days during a waxing moon. Choose a candle in a color that corresponds with whatever you are wishing to manifest. For instance, you might choose a green candle if you're hoping to manifest money or a brown candle if you're hoping to find the perfect new animal companion. If it's a new romance you're after, you might pick a red or pink candle to symbolize love and affection or purple to symbolize passion or a spiritual connection. Begin by tracing on the ground or on your lunar altar a large circle with your fingertip or wand tip. Think of the spherical moon as you trace the shape, and imagine that the design you are making is expanding in three dimensions to create an orb of energy. Think of this as a replica of the moon itself, a mini model you have constructed that contains all the essence and vibrations of its much larger real-life counterpart. Arrange around this circle three clear quartz crystals, two at the top and one at the bottom in a triangle formation, their tips pointing inward toward the middle of the circle. Now turn your attentions to the candle. Using a needle or straight pin, carve into the candle wax, starting at the top and working your way toward the middle, words or symbols to describe what you wish to manifest. Keep it simple. If you're wanting more wealth, you can simply carve the word "money" into the candle or trace a dollar sign. You might write the same word or symbol over and over again, spiraling down the length of the candle. If you like, anoint the candle with vanilla or coconut oil. Place the candle in the middle of the circle and light it. Envision the resources you want manifesting before your eyes as you chant:

I call upon this circle whole!

Help me to achieve my goal!

Moon so bright and crystals clear,

Share your might, and bring it here!

Bring to me the things I seek!

Bring it here within a week!

Let the candle burn all the way down to end the spell, or let it burn for a while and extinguish it, repeating the ritual on the following nights until the candle is entirely consumed. Leave the crystals and candle remnants in place until your desired resources have manifested.

• • • SPELL 31 • • •
Money Spell

Try this spell to increase your wealth. Place a round mirror on the ground or on your altar under the light of the moon. Invite the energies of the moon to enter the mirror, and imagine the moonlight melding itself into the shiny glass. Arrange upon the mirror a ring of thirteen one-dollar bills, quarters, or silver coins. Gaze into the mirror as you say these words and imagine yourself blessed with wealth:

My wealth shines and reflects like the moon in the heaven!

Each dollar I spend will return back as seven!

Each dollar I save will attract even more!

May currency magnified flow through my door!

Honey moon!

Money moon!

Bring wealth to me, and bring it soon!

Honey moon!

Money moon!

Bring wealth to me, and bring it soon!

Open your heart in welcome as you envision and invite a greater flow of wealth to enter your life. Imagine yourself sharing your wealth with others and doing good things with the abundant flow of money that is on its way to you. Smile at your reflection, then take the money off the mirror and put it all into an envelope marked on the outside with thirteen dollar signs drawn in a circle. Put the mirror away, as it is no longer needed in the magic. Give some of the money away, spend some, and save some to finish setting the spell into motion.

chapter seven

Obstacle Removal Spell 1

Use this quick and easy charm to help clear away obstacles to your progress forward. On a night when clouds are drifting across the sky, obscuring then revealing the face of the moon, cast this charm. Stand outside when clouds are covering your view of the moon, and think of the obstacles that hinder you. Say to yourself, "Those are not clouds, but my obstacles that hide the light of the moon!" With your lips pursed toward the sky, blow gently as you think of those obstacles drifting away, scattering easily at the force of your command. As the clouds begin to drift away and reveal the shining moon, say, "I blow away my obstacles! As the moon is revealed, so too is my path forward cleared!" Gaze at the unobstructed moon and envision yourself moving forward with ease, exhaling or blowing slowly as you imagine any obstacles in your path scattering and disappearing into the cosmos.

Obstacle Removal Spell 2

You'll need a small piece of paper, a pen, a black candle, a set of tongs, a fireproof dish, and a cup of water. Write on a small piece of paper a description of the obstacle you would like to remove or conquer. Holding it with the tongs over the fireproof dish, burn this paper in the flame of a black candle outside under a setting moon. Scatter the ashes into a straight line. Step over the line of ashes as you say, "I step over this obstacle easily." Blow on the ashes or sweep them away with a broom so that they scatter. Say, "I sweep away this obstacle with ease." Pour the cup of water all over the area and say, "I wash away any traces of this obstacle. There is nothing that stands in my way!"

• • • SPELL 34 • • •
Peace Spell

Use this spell to help end conflict and to promote feelings of peace and compassion. Fill a bowl with coconut water (or regular water with an additional ingredient to encourage harmony and friendship, such as basil or vanilla). Think of this bowl as representing the moon. Alternate between gazing into the liquid in the bowl, and gazing up at the moon (or imagining the moon in your mind's eye, if you're doing the spell indoors). Breathe slowly and fully as you do your best to clear your own energy, exhaling any tension, anxiety, and anger, and expanding your inner space with each inhalation. When you feel as calm and clear as possible, think of the serene feeling that observing the moon can bring, and let this tranquil energy flow from your heart and flow from the moon and into the bowl. Now look at your hands, and think of each of them as representing the parties between which you wish to bring peace. You might draw a symbol on each hand, or write a name if it helps you to envision this. If you prefer, use two flowers instead to symbolize the individuals between which you wish to make peace. Place your hands—or alternatively, the two flowers—into the bowl of coconut water, sliding them together through the peaceful water blessed by the moon. Grasp your hands together under the water, or if you're using flowers instead, bring the two flowers together so that they are side by side in the middle of the bowl. Envision a peaceful scene of positive communication and mutual compassion. You might imagine the parties shaking hands, or perhaps laughing together or working side by side to successfully complete a project. You can chant this verse to help strengthen the expression of your will and intention:

Strife decrease!
Goodwill increase!
Mother Moon!
Make a path for peace!
(repeat three times)

Pour the water around the base of a tree or in a flower bed.

• • • SPELL 35 • • •
Petitioning the Dead Spell

If you would like to utilize your lunar connection to gain the aid of the dead, try this spell to petition the dearly departed for a helping hand.

If there isn't a particular spirit you are wishing to work with, you might try carrying out this spell in a graveyard for the best chance of gaining the attentions of the dead. Go outside where you can clearly see the moon. Focus your thoughts on the spirit or spirits you are wishing to call forth. Think of the moon as a giant transmitter, ready to broadcast your "signal" throughout the heavens. Express your wishes to the moon. Invite the spirit or spirits to come to you, repeating their name and fervently requesting that they come to your aid. If you like, use this verse to ask for the moon's assistance in calling on the dead:

> Great light that reveals there is life after death!
>
> Light after darkness!
>
> Life after death!

Make a path through the dark,

make a path made of light!

Tell the dead to come forward,

come to me tonight!

I call on a soul that you hold in your heart.

I ask of you, moon, for your help to impart!

Bring forward the one that I name here tonight;

bring forward this one in a body of light!

State the full name of the person, saying after the name the words, "I call you forward! I ask of you to come to me, here, now!" Repeat this request until you feel their presence. If you're not able to make contact, try another spirit or try again at another time.

Once you feel that the dead are in your presence, think deeply about the issue that is troubling you, and ask clearly for exactly the aid you wish the spirit to render on your behalf. Write your request on a small piece of paper, then roll it up tightly. Tie a piece of red thread around the middle to hold it together. Leave the scroll at the gravesite of the spirit you're petitioning. You can alternatively place it in a dark space such as a hollow log, bury it underground, or tuck it amongst the tree roots.

The moon is on average a scorching 260 degrees Fahrenheit (127 degrees Celsius) when in full sun, but in darkness, the lunar temperature plummets to about -280 degrees Fahrenheit!

• • • SPELL 36 • • •
Prosperity Spell

Try this spell to increase the flow of money coming to you. Trace a large circle on a piece of paper around the time of the first appearance of the new moon. On the first day, fill in a tiny crescent-shaped sliver of the circle with dollar signs or another money symbol drawn in red or green ink. Each day, carry on the process a bit further, filling in as much of the circle as you can see of the moon. After you draw the symbols, rub a piece of basalt over them, imagining that you are charging up these symbols with an attractive force that will pull the money to you like a magnet. The darker areas visible on the moon's surface— called the lunar maria, or lunar seas—were formed from ancient volcanic eruptions. Think of the piece of basalt that you hold as being linked to the basalt on the moon and know that just as the moon is able to pull the oceans toward it, so too can you draw to yourself the money that you desire. Repeat this process on each consecutive night until the moon is full and your circle is entirely filled in with dollar signs. On the night of the full moon, cover the image you have made with shiny coins. Let this sit out under the full moon, the piece of basalt sitting on top of the coins at the middle of the image. Before the sun rises, pour the coins into a pouch, and wrap the paper around the basalt. Put this in the pouch along with the coins. As soon as possible, give all but one of the coins away. Keep the paper, the basalt, and a single coin in the pouch and keep this in your purse, wallet, bag, or pocket. When you receive extra or unexpected money, tuck some of it into this pouch to help attract more of the same.

• • • SPELL 37 • • •
Protection Spell

Take a photo of the person you wish to protect and place this on top of a mirror or a piece of white cloth. If you don't have a photo of the person, you can substitute with a small piece of paper on which you have written the person's full name. If you are able to obtain a piece of hair from the person you are wishing to protect, you might place this on the photo or on top of their name. Next, charge a moonstone with the light of the moon, asking for and willing the moon's power to flow into the stone. Envision the energies inherent in the moonstone reaching out for and connecting with the energies streaming from the moon. Once the moonstone is ready, place it on the mirror or white cloth, just above the person's name or photo. Use your finger to glide the moonstone in a circle that encompasses the photo or name, making a total of thirteen complete rotations. After the last rotation, place the moonstone directly on top of the photo or name, and leave this in place until the immediate need for extra protection has passed.

• • • SPELL 38 • • •
Psychic Awareness Spell

Use this quick spell to open, activate, and enhance your psychic awareness. Outside under the moonlight, hold a moonstone gently against your forehead, just above and between your eyes where the third eye chakra—center of psychic consciousness—is said to be located. Try to focus on the energy residing at this place in your body. See if you can envision the energy there swirling around, faster and faster. Invite the energies of the moon to come down into the moonstone and into your own energetic aura, bringing with it illumination that expands your awareness. Take the moonstone off your forehead now, but continue to hold it in your hand. Envision the swirling energy of your third-eye chakra expanding outward, opening what looks like a large doorway in the center of this ring of swirling power. Open that doorway and receive whatever impressions may come. Keep the moonstone nearby whenever you are engaging in psychic work, or carry it with you close to your body to help boost the overall growth of your psychic ability.

• • • SPELL 39 • • •
Revelation Spell

Use this spell to gain a fresh perspective on a perplexing issue. Take a deck of tarot cards outside under the moon. Pull out the Moon card and place this before you. Place beneath this the rest of your tarot deck. Gaze at the moon for a while and let these energies flow into you. Invite these energies to flow also into your tarot cards. Mix the cards in a loose heap as you think about the issue that's troubling you. Now make a fist and hold your hand up to your eye as if it's a periscope. Gaze at the moon through the small opening in your fist. If you happen to have a fairy stone (a rock with a hole naturally worn through it) or a seashell with a naturally formed hole in it, you can use that instead to the same effect. Gaze at the moon and let your eyes relax. See if you can relax into a trance state that will induce visions. If you're not quite able to get into a trance, still pay attention to any sensations or impressions that might come to you during your moon-gazing. When you're finished, turn your attention back to your tarot cards. Notice the moonlight shining down on your cards and think of this light as having the power to illuminate. You can say this rhyme to petition the moon for further assistance, or put your request into your own words:

All-knowing moon!
All-seeing moon!
Help me to know!
Help me to see!
Show me what is hidden!
Reveal to me the truth I seek!
Reveal to me what I should see!
Show me, moon!
Know me, moon!
Bring the light of truth to me!

With your eyes on the moon, touch your pile of tarot cards and choose any that seem to stand out to you. Interpret these cards for insights into the matter you are wanting to know about. Note your dreams over the course of the next few nights after performing this spell, as information and insights might take a little time to reveal themselves.

• • • SPELL 40 • • •
Strength Spell

Use this spell to boost your sense of courage and inner
strength whenever you are doubting yourself. Prepare
for this spell by thinking of an animal you can relate to,
one which you perceive as being strong in the way that
you desire. You might choose a crocodile for its fearsome
qualities, or perhaps a bear for its mighty strength. You
might choose a wolf for its alertness and vigilance of
defense. You might consider a less obvious selection like
a turtle, for instance, due to its inherent ability to protect itself. Choose an animal that you like and that fits
your purpose of symbolizing the type of strength you
are wishing to renew or acquire. The action of this spell
requires you to imagine yourself as this animal, so to help
along that process, you might want to draw an image of
the chosen animal on your body or even dress in animal
mask or other costumery. You might also use drawings,
photos, or figurines of the animal to act as
a focal point. A stuffed animal representation of the selected creature can also be an
excellent addition. When you're ready to
begin, think of the strong qualities of the
animal you have chosen. Imagine that animal

exhibiting those traits, seeing it in your mind's eye from the perspective of the observer. Feel your admiration for the animal's strength and worth. Now shift your perspective so that you are envisioning the scene through the eyes of the animal. Try to contain your consciousness within this animal body, and imagine the animal body expanding, growing larger than life. Imagine yourself as the animal exhibiting tremendous strength. Feel your body as if it is a giant-sized version of the animal's body. Imagine an incredible power radiating out from this enormous body and reaching out toward the energies of the moon, that are in turn reaching out toward you. Imagine that these streams of energy are overlapping, connecting, weaving themselves together. Think of the power of the moon, pulling on the waters of the ocean. Imagine yourself having this power, drawing the oceans toward you with a wave of your hands. Think of the moon alerting nocturnal animals that it is time to wake up, and warning diurnal animals that it's time to take cover and rest. Imagine yourself having this power over the world's many beasts. Feel your energies connected with the strength of the moon, and focus on drawing these energies into your body that you are still imagining in larger-than-life animal form. As you reach your maximum for absorbing the lunar flow, envision your body slowly returning back to ordinary shape and size, but keeping within that physical framework all the strength and power of the moon and the animal that you just invoked.

• • • SPELL 41 • • •
Success Spell

Success means different things to each of us. When working a spell for general success, it's important to define for yourself what success actually means to you. What does it look like? What does it feel like? Exactly what outcome are you hoping to achieve? You might not be sure exactly what needs to happen, but you know you could use an extra boost of luck to help open the right doors for you moving forward. Whatever sort of success you are going for, you can utilize the moon to help manifest your wishes. Choose a time when the moon is in a waxing phase in a sign conducive to the type of success you are going for. Write down on a small piece of paper a description of the success you're after. Be as clear and concise as possible, stating your desire in positive terms that describe the outcome you desire as if it has already become reality. Place this paper under a clear glass bowl filled with water. In the bowl, place a moonstone. Also place in the bowl a floating candle. Light the candle as you focus your thoughts on the moon, then on your vision for success. Surround the candle with thirteen small white flowers or flower petals, placing them one at a time as you make a wish on the moon for success. Express your wishes in your own words, and add some praise for the moon with each wish. For example, you might say something like: "Powerful moon that moves the waters of the earth, please help me move mountains and grant me success!" Let the bowl sit under the moonlight for as long as you can. Don't leave the candle burning unattended, and finish up before the sun rises. Remove the candle and scoop out the flowers. Place the flowers on the ground in a circle and leave them there. Pour the water along with the moonstone into a bottle or jar. Tape the paper on which you wrote your description of your wish for success onto the outside of the container, but facing inward so that the words you wrote are facing the liquid. On the outward facing side of the paper, draw an image of the moon. You might draw a full moon, a waxing moon, or a triple moon symbol. Use this potion to anoint your own body or any significant objects or tools you will use in your quest for success. For example, if your intention is to become a successful artist, you might anoint your paint brushes and canvas with the potion, and maybe dab some on your wrists or forehead before you begin your artwork.

• • • SPELL 42 • • •
Temper-Reducing Spell

If you're feeling irritable, try this spell to help soothe your nerves and calm your mind. Fill a glass with cold water and take it outside under the moonlight. Rub the glass gently across your forehead as you say:

Calm moon, cool moon!

Peaceful and serene moon!

As you temper the sunlight,

Temper my nerves!

Diffuse what is harsh!

Disperse what is sharp!

Make me calm and cool,

Like your heavenly light!

Drink the water and breathe deeply for a few moments as you envision yourself taking in the fresh, cool light of the moon.

Tranquility Ritual

This ritual can bring tranquility when you're feeling anxious or unsettled. Ideally, perform this ritual outside where you can see the moon. Choose a plate or a small shallow box, and fill it with a mound of sand. You'll also need a selection of lunar stones. You might choose moonstone, quartz crystal, obsidian, aquamarine, serpentine, or any round or crescent shaped white or gray stone. Use a small twig, a paint brush, or a fork to gently spread the sand in an even layer. As you spread the sand, think of the action of the moon on the ocean, turning the tides that broke up the rocks that produced the very sand you now have right at your fingertips. Imagine the ocean waves rolling in and out, back and forth, swaying in rhythm with the motion of the moon. Take some time to trace some designs in the sand that appeal to you. You might make spiral shapes, trace a labyrinth, or create rows of symmetrical ridges. You might create some mini craters to mimic the surface of the moon. Now think of yourself, a tiny creature on a planet that in the whole scheme of the incomprehensibly vast universe, is itself rather tiny. Arrange some of the rocks you have chosen one by one on the surface of the sand as you think about yourself and other people or things in nature that you love, standing here on this earth with you, spinning through space as the moon spins around us and our solar system spins around the galaxy.

Think of all the humans and animals throughout the ages that have gazed up at the moon and found solace there in the earth's steadfast companion. It can feel very lonely in this massive universe, but somehow knowing that our planet has a partner on our journey through the galaxy helps us to not feel quite so alone. Perhaps it's the desolation of the moon, the loneliness of the moon that rather than causing chaos and upset, creates an unshakeable peace and tranquility, the sense of knowing one's place in the universe and owning our own space without the need for any outside validation, approval, or understanding. Now add more stones as you think of the feeling of peace and harmony that you wish to experience. If you like, as you place each stone, you might think of something you wish to welcome more of into your life. Spend as much time as you like playing with the sand and the rocks as you let the energies of the moon above flow into you. Leave your design outdoors or on your altar to rearrange the next time you're feeling on edge.

• • • SPELL 43 • • •

Transformation Spell

This is a good spell to do when you're feeling the need to shift your energies. Try timing this one to coincide with the moon's transit into a house you feel is favorable for your current pursuits and the type of shift you are going for. For instance, if you have been feeling bored, doing this spell as the moon moves into Scorpio, the place of passion and excitement, could be particularly beneficial. If you've felt as if you've been a bit too withdrawn emotionally and you want to open up to being more sensitive, you might try casting the spell as the moon transits into Cancer, ruler of emotions. Whenever you choose to work the spell, you'll need two large pieces of quartz crystal (preferably imperfect as they will get marred and banged up a bit during this working), and a set of safety glasses or goggles to protect your eyes. Take the crystals outside if you can, in a dark area where there isn't a lot of light pollution. If you can't

The Chinese poet Li Bai wrote many famous poems about the moon.

get away from the city lights where you live, you can do the spell indoors, but take care to put a drop cloth down in the area so that it will be easier to clean up any crystal fragments that may potentially become dislodged. Put on your eye protection. Hold the crystals, one in each hand, upward toward the moon. Envision that lunar energy being drawn into the crystals. Feel in your body the essence of the moon's vibrations, and see the moon clearly in your mind's eye. Consciously draw this energy toward you and into the crystals. Imagine a connecting thread of this energy forming between the two crystals. Now focus your thoughts on the transformation that you would like to occur. You might choose a simple image to symbolize this transformation, such as a moth, a blooming lotus, or the moon reemerging from behind a cloud, or rising up from the horizon. Think of this visual symbol and imagine this image placed on the connecting thread of lunar energy running from crystal to crystal. If you like, use these words of petition to help express your intention for the magical working:

Ever-changing moon!
Ever-moving moon!
From light to dark and dark to light!

Shifting shadows in the night!

Changing all with lunar light!

Share with me, moon,

your mighty might!

Change this situation!

Transform this circumstance!

No more can the current way remain!

A new way must be forged today on this very night!

I hereby make a path for this new way!

With the sway of the moon, this new road is cut!

With the light of the moon, this new trail is blazed!

With the power of the moon, it will always remain!

From the path of my thoughts

to the mountains of the moon,

a new way is formed,

transformation comes soon!

Now relax your arms and hold the crystals by your sides with the points facing downwards toward the ground. Bring the crystals together in front of you, but angle them down and away from your body. Begin rubbing the crystals together vigorously, one on the other, taking care to keep them pointed down and away from you, in case any shards fly off. After a few seconds, the friction will cause a piezoelectric effect in the crystals that will make them give off a luminous glow. If it's not happening, try rubbing the crystals in a different spot, or increasing the friction. When the crystals are glowing, keep visualizing the symbol of transformation you selected, and in your mind's eye, see this symbol superimposed over the glowing crystals. When you feel you have raised the energy to the maximum and are visualizing your desired transformation clearly, project the energy you have raised to flow out from the crystals and upwards toward the moon. You might instead put the crystals in a special pouch or box to keep nearby to help support your transformation process, particularly if you expect this transformation will be particularly lengthy or intense. If that's the case, don't release the energy out of the crystals at the pinnacle of the spell; instead, direct all the energy raised to be bound into the crystals that are linked through your visualization to your spell's intention.

• • • SPELL 44 • • •
Wisdom Spell

If you are seeking to advance your wisdom and open your mind to new knowledge and insight, try this spell. You'll need a piece of jade, preferably smooth and relatively flat on one side. Set this stone outside under the moonlight or near a window where it can catch the moonrays. Near the stone, place a white, dark blue, golden yellow, or gray candle. Take a few moments to clear your head before you focus your thoughts on the moon. Think of its size, its rotation upon its axis, its orbit around the earth and around the sun. Visualize these movements taking place again and again, advancing time while encapsulating the eternal, immune to the petty and indifferent to the whims of fate. Think of the light of the sun falling upon the moon and reflecting that light upon us. Light the candle as you let the feeling of the moon's glowing light expand within you. Place your fingertips upon the jade as you invite the moon to pour its timeless wisdom into the stone. You can use these words to assist you:

Moon so big and moon so bright,
expand my sight!
Expand my sight!
Unlock my mind so I will know
the mysteries beyond your glow.
Bring to me wisdom!
Bring to me light!
Expand my sight and make it bright!
Bring to me wisdom!

Bring to me light!

Expand my sight and make it bright!

Gaze into the candle flame and open your mind to whatever thoughts and images might enter into it. When you feel that you've received all the insights you're going to receive in that way, extinguish the candle. Then, take some additional time to sit in a comfortable reclined position or lie down, and place the jade stone upon your forehead. Close your eyes and again let your thoughts flow naturally. Pay attention to whatever comes to mind. When you are finished, get a pen and some paper and have a quick brainstorming session to jot down any new ideas or problem-solving possibilities that may occur to you. Keep the jade stone close to your body or use it as a focal point for meditation or to help your mind absorb knowledge when you are studying to learn something new.

• • •

Chapter Eight

A YEAR OF
MOON MAGIC

Here, you'll find a guide to making moon magic throughout the year with seasonally-themed lunar spells and correspondences that reflect and celebrate Nature's changing tides. You'll find a description of the general energy flow for each month, as well as a list of seasonal lunar symbols including a full moon spell, and a dark moon or new moon spell for each month. If you live in the Southern Hemisphere, your seasonal energy flow will be very different; simply add six months to the months listed here so that the symbolism will accurately reflect your local seasons. For example, March's listing here will apply to September in the Southern Hemisphere, while December's listing will apply to June in the Southern Hemisphere. By working with the moon throughout the year, you'll strengthen your magic as well as your lunar connection and understanding.

January

January can often be a very trying month, especially for those of us who yearn for the longer, brighter days ahead. Nature has turned inward and so have we, so it's possible we feel as though we're frozen from the inside out! The start of the new year coinciding with the start of January can seem an odd juxtaposition; just as we are feeling like all we want to do is cuddle up under a blanket and hide out until springtime, the world is inviting us to embrace a new beginning, to pledge our allegiance to a fresh set of the loftiest hopes and goals imaginable that we're willing to pursue with unwavering dedication and ambition. It's a tall order, and we are not obligated to fulfill it. There is a lot of pressure from society at this time of year to adopt the so-called New Year's Resolution, infamous for its inevitable failure and typically focused on what a person is vowing to never do, rather than being focused on what one wishes to do. We don't have to allow self-shaming and peer pressure to be the motivating factors, however. Finding our own ways to joyfully mark the start of the new year and optimistically set our sights on the success we desire can bring advantages by raising our vibrations in a way that helps us stay strong and vibrant through winter's depths. The energy of celebration and new beginnings that dominates the atmosphere of the start of the new year can be a very beneficial fuel for your magic throughout the month of January. It's a good time to reevaluate your dreams and work a little magic to make those dreams come true. It's also a good time to strengthen protections and fortify defenses so that you can head into the new year with greater confidence and courage.

SEASONAL LUNAR SYMBOLS: Ice, snow, grapes, wine

COLORS: White, silver, gray, black

ANIMAL: Wolf, snowy owl

FOLK NAMES: Wolf Moon, Spirit Moon, Old Moon, Ice Moon

Full Moon Spell for a Successful Year

The first full moon of the year affords a wonderful opportunity to solidify your intentions for growth and evolution in the new year ahead. If you prefer, you might perform this spell on New Year's Eve or on the night of January 1st, whatever phase the moon may be in at that time. You'll need a small round mirror and a silver or white candle for this spell. Hold the candle in your hands and think about your wishes for the year to come. Visualize the success you wish to receive, and more importantly, do your best to vividly imagine and feel the emotional sensations in your body that you will experience when your vision comes true. Build this energy as much as you can so that it emanates and extends well beyond your physical form. Know that this energy is within your control and command, and you can direct and project this energy to flow into whatever channels you wish in order to make the connections in the astral between what you wish for, and the underlying thread of vibration which can bring it. To be most effective, visualizations need to be emotionally charged with the feeling you will get when your desires are manifested. Look up at the moon, then light the candle as you imagine this being the spark that sets in motion the forces to carry out your magical intention. Hold the small mirror in front of you and gaze at your face. Tell yourself that this is a face that deserves success. Imagine that all your best dreams have come true. Smile confidently at your reflection, then place the mirror on a flat surface and leave it outside under the moonlight to soak up the magical power of the full moon which will help magnify the effect of your spell. Retrieve the mirror before sunrise. You can carry the mirror with you, or keep it in a special place in your home. Look in the mirror throughout the year to remind you to have confidence in your abilities to manifest your dreams.

• • • SPELL 46 • • •
New Moon Spell for Protection of Self and Home

Take a piece of onyx and place it outside or on your altar following the new moon's reemergence. Surround the onyx with a circle of smaller pieces of onyx, one for each member of your household. Place to the west of the onyx a white candle to symbolize the waxing moon, place to the east of the onyx a black candle to symbolize the waning moon, and to the north of the onyx place a red candle to symbolize the full moon. Light each candle with a separate match, and place the matches so that they lay in between the candles with their burnt tips facing outward, away from the onyx. Think of the triangular formation of the candles and the lunar energies it represents like a shield, protecting your home and yourself and your family. Think of the strength and durability of the onyx, invulnerable and unshakable. Think of the burnt match tips driving away and banishing any dangers or negativity that threatens to come near. Imagine concentric orbs of protective energy surrounding yourself, each member of your family, and your home. Imagine these protective orbs growing in strength and power as you also envision the new moon growing in size to become a full moon. Place your fingertips on the center piece of onyx as you do so. You can use the verse below to seal the charm, or simply end with the visualization, projecting the energy of the spell into the piece of onyx in the center, and imagining that energy radiating outward into the smaller pieces of onyx, as well:

Every culture on earth has its own lore and legends surrounding the moon.

May the protection of the moon
be upon me and my home!
May the moon watch over me and mine
wherever we may roam!
(repeat three times)

Place the largest piece of onyx somewhere near the "heart" of your home, be that near the fireplace, in the living room, or in the kitchen—wherever the family tends to gather and feel most comfortable. Give each family member one of the smaller onyx pieces and take one yourself to keep on your person as a protective charm. Bury or hide each of the burnt matches around the outside of your property. Place one by the front entrance, perhaps tucked behind the back edge of the doormat, or concealed behind a large potted plant or piece of statuary. Place the other two on each of the back corners of the dwelling. Conceal the matchsticks or cover them with a thin layer of dirt. You don't want them covered so well that their magic won't work as intended, but you also don't want them totally exposed to view. As you place the matches, imagine that each one has a repelling quality that will send away any unwanted dangers that would otherwise threaten the home.

• • •

February

With February comes the first whispers and promise of warmer days to come—eventually, anyway! The days are continuing to grow longer little by little, and we can feel the vibrant energies of the earth begin to stir and awaken beneath the surface. It becomes a little easier to find our motivation, and we find our inner strength increasing as we begin to shake off the dark cloak of winter's depths. Purification magic is especially effective at this time, as is love, lust, and romance magic. With Valentine's Day plastering the world with reminders that love is something to celebrate, February is a fine time for spells to attract love and increase the passions. The ancient Roman festival of Lupercalia was held in February, and it was a time to celebrate lust and fertility.

SEASONAL LUNAR SYMBOLS: Ice, mirror, springs, wells, white rose

COLORS: White, red, purple

ANIMALS: White cow, wolf, snake

FOLK NAMES: Snow Moon, Hunger Moon, Storm Moon

• • • SPELL 47 • • •

Full Moon Spell to Attract Love

Perform this full moon spell outside near a well, stream, ocean, or other water source. (If this isn't possible, you can substitute an empowered bowl of water; just pour the water outdoors once the spell is complete.) Stand under the moonlight and call on the moon to witness your act. Tuck a piece of your hair into the blossom of a white rose while envisioning the sort of lover you wish to attract, and imagining the feelings in your body and soul that this lover will bring to you. Gently brush your fingertips along the petals as you invite the energies of the moon to lend their power to your magic, envisioning these energies being drawn into the rose as you touch it. Then lock your eyes on the full moon as you toss the rose into the water as you make your wish for love.

• • • SPELL 48 • • •

New Moon Spell for Purification

At the time of the dark moon, use this spell to help rid yourself of any baneful, negative, or otherwise harmful energies and constructs that you feel are holding you back from achieving your potential. Hold an ice cube in your hand and think about it as if it is a little chunk of moon energy, full of a serene and purifying power that can cleanse away unwanted energy just as easily as it can cause ocean waves to sweep away the sand. Ask for the energies of the moon to enter into the ice cube. Rub the ice cube over your face and hands as you envision pushing out of your body any negative energies you wish to be rid of. Imagine a bright and powerful energy at the core of your being, and expand this energy so that it pushes out the undesired energies. Envision these unwanted energies going into the ice. Now light a white candle and hold this in one hand tilted slightly toward the horizontal, over a fire-proof surface that can catch the wax. With your other hand, waft the ice cube through the flame, taking care that the water from the melting ice doesn't drip onto the candle wick and put it out. You don't need to melt the ice completely in this way. Just pass it a few times through the flame or hold it near enough so that you can watch it drip a bit. As you do so, think of the way that the illuminating sunlight reflects off the surface of the moon, and how the light of the moon grows and returns following its apparent plunge into darkness. Imagine yourself being lit up with light just as the moon will be as it grows over the next stage of its monthly journey. Leave the remaining ice on a dish placed on your altar or near a fireplace indoors until it melts, or place it outside to melt if the weather is warm enough. Pour the water from the melted ice onto a wild growing plant. As another option, you can take the ice cube outdoors and smash it with a hammer over a hard surface as you envision the negative energy you willed out of your body and into the ice shattering and disintegrating as you do so.

• • •

March

The month of the Spring Equinox, March is a time of massive energy shifts. Nature is switching gears as it finds a new balance, and our external and internal worlds are in a state of flux as we too adjust to the shifting seasonal tides. You can expect the unexpected to happen in March. It's a time to stay alert and be mindful, but it's also a time to let your guard down enough to ride the waves of excitable, unpredictable energy with optimism and courage. Fear can be very paralyzing and inhibiting, even if the dangers we fear are anticipated dangers that aren't actually occurring, and may or may not ever occur. Nonetheless, it can be hard to shake a sense of anxiety and dread off of one's heart when the world itself seems to be in a state of rapid change conducive to unlikely happenings. Unexpected obstacles, unforeseen dangers, and freak accidents are indeed potential perils, but this is in fact always the case. If you find yourself entering the month of March with an uneasy feeling, don't be surprised. This is a time when we reaffirm or recreate the foundations upon which we stand, adjusting our footing so to speak until we find that place where we again feel centered, balanced, and grounded. It's a good time to work magic to help fortify your courage and strengthen your protections as you open yourself to the positive and fortunate unexpected possibilities that the quickening, invigorating energies of spring can bring.

SEASONAL LUNAR SYMBOLS: Three-leaf clovers, half-moon or crescent shaped rocks, eggs, egg-shaped rocks, coins, smooth, round shiny stones

COLORS: White, green

ANIMALS: Rabbits, frogs, snakes

FOLK NAMES: Worm Moon, Sap Moon, Crow Moon

Full Moon Spell for Courage and Protection

Place a mirror on a flat, stable surface outside or near a window so that it can soak up the full moon energy. Choose a small silver object such as a ring, pendant, or coin, and place this in the center of the mirror. To the east of the silver object, place a piece of amethyst. To the south, place a piece of obsidian. To the west, place a piece of aquamarine. Above the silver, place a piece of quartz crystal, and above the quartz, place a moonstone. Gaze at your reflection in the mirror, partially covered by the silver object and surrounded by the lunar-attuned stones that are all radiating with beneficial, protective, powerful energies. Imagine yourself protected and strong, guarded by an impenetrable light that shines so brightly from within you that no dangers or darkness can breach your barriers. You can use these words if needed to help focus your will:

> With the earth in my heart, with the moon above me!
>
> With the moon and the earth in my body and soul!
>
> With the fire in my belly and the wind at my back!
>
> I stand with nature while my foes stand alone!
>
> With the power of the oceans behind me!

With the strength of the earth beneath me!

With the strength of the moon above me!

With the strength of the wild things beside me!

I stand with Nature while my foes stand alone!

All my enemies blown away, all my obstacles reduced to ashes!

All impurities washed away, all dangers buried in the dirt!

I stand with Nature while my foes stand alone!

I have the protection of the elements!

I have the protection of the earth and moon!

I am protected from all danger!

I face the world with a heart of courage!

While my foes stand alone,

I stand with Nature!

I stand with Nature, between the earth and the moon!

Gather the stones and the silver object into a dark green or light gray cloth and tie it up with a silver or white ribbon. (Depending on the silver item you chose to use, you can include it in the bundle with the stones, or if it's a ring or another piece of jewelry, you may prefer to keep it separate so that you can wear it instead.) Draw a circle on the bundle to represent the full moon. Once the bundle is made, hold it in your hand and repeat this verse as you envision the energies of the stones being further charged and magnified by the energies of the full moon:

> My guiding light, the full moon's glow,
>
> I flawlessly will ride the flow!
>
> (repeat three times)

Carry this bundle with you for protection and courage.

• • • SPELL 50 • • •
New Moon Spell for Good Luck

This spell will help attract good fortune and increase the potential for positive and enjoyable occurrences. Work this magic when the new moon can be observed as a waxing crescent settling down toward the horizon shortly after sunset. Find or make a figurine or other token bearing the likeness and shape of a rabbit, and anoint this image with jasmine oil. Hold a quartz crystal above the rabbit's head and rub the crystal between your thumb and other fingers as you imagine yourself experiencing a windfall of good luck. Imagine the energy of your thoughts combining with the energies of the moon and flowing into the crystal, then into the rabbit. Place the crystal before the rabbit, and focus your attention on the moon. Notice how the moon's crescent shape might be seen as a cup, ready to scoop up all the good things you wish for. Cup your hands together as if you are gathering within them the moonlight, and act as if you are drinking this up as you imagine yourself soaking in the power and energy of the moonlight. Leave the crystal somewhere outside in the open air, but in a place where it is unlikely to be found. Carry the rabbit with you or keep it prominently placed in your home, preferably near the entrance.

• • •

April

April is a time of nourishment and rejuvenation as many places on earth experience a sharp increase in moisture and rapidly warming temperatures. It's an ideal time for embracing and embarking on those new beginnings you may have envisioned back in January, but perhaps haven't quite gotten around to making them happen just yet. It's also a good time to count your blessings, nourish relationships, and invite more love into your life.

SEASONAL LUNAR SYMBOLS: Eggs, egg-shaped stones, smooth, round white stones, raindrop shapes, bubbles

COLORS: White, silver, light green, pale gray, pastel blue

ANIMALS: Small birds, rabbits, ducks

FOLK NAMES: Pink Moon, Egg Moon, Hare Moon, Sprouting Grass Moon

• • • SPELL 51 • • •

Full Moon Spell for Abundant Love

Use this spell to help open your heart to giving and receiving an abundant flow of love. Sometimes, we may have trouble feeling that we are worthy of love, especially if our hearts have been mistreated. The first step in opening your heart to a greater flow of love is to feel that you deserve that love, and to do so you must be willing to give to yourself the nourishment of the same compassion that you show to others. This spell will help you to nourish your heart so that love can thrive there. It can also be used to help encourage a budding love to blossom and flourish, or to help a long-existing but neglected love spring back to life. Obtain some white flower seeds or some seeds from a night-blossoming flower such as night-blooming jasmine or evening primrose. You'll need either a large planter or an appropriate place in your yard or garden in which to plant the seeds. Under a full moon, prepare the soil for the seeds as you invite the energies of the moon to enter into the earth as you mix it and loosen it. When you're ready, gently smooth over the top layer of the soil and trace upon it a heart shape using your fingertip or wand tip, while holding your other hand over your heart. Imagine the loving feeling that you wish to share in greater abundance, and let this emotion swell beyond your heart so that it flows through your body and into the soil. Hold the seeds in your open hand and let the moonlight flow into them. Close your hand over the seeds and hold them close to your heart as you imagine how it would feel to have a more abundant flow of love in your life. Imagine that emotion and energy of love surrounding you in a comforting orb of light. Now in this safe space, envision that you are literally opening a space within your heart, expanding it or creating a gateway through which a current of love is invited to take course. Let this emotion and energy of love flow from your heart and soul, through the seeds, to the moon and back and out to the great beyond, raining back upon the earth like a nourishing rain. Next, arrange the seeds within the heart-shaped groove that you made in the soil. In the middle of the heart, place a moonstone. Think of the moon as being connected to the moonstone, and imagine threads of lunar energy flowing into the stone and radiating outward to enter into each and every seed. Gently smooth the soil over the seeds, and pat it down. Use

MOON BEARS

Moon bears are a species of black bear native to the forests and mountainous regions of southeast Asia. With a large, cream-colored crescent moon shaped marking across their chests, shaggy fur, and elongated ears, these Asiatic black bears spend much of their time in the trees. In upland regions of Japan, local legends ascribe the moon bear's unusual crescent-shaped marking to a magical amulet that was given to the bear by Yama-no-Kami, a mountain deity. The amulet was so powerful that it left on the bear a permanent mark of Yama-no-Kami's protection.

a watering can to carefully sprinkle some water over the soil and upon the moonstone, doing so with a loving heart as you think of how the love you are able to feel and share is every bit as nourishing as the rain.

New Moon Spell for New Beginnings

Select a time for your spell when you will most likely be available to catch your first glimpse of the new moon after it reappears as the thinnest waxing crescent, following the several days when it's not at all visible. Go outside at this time, taking care to keep your back turned toward the moon so as not to see it just yet. Stand quietly with the moon behind you and think about the new beginning on which you would like to embark. Think about taking those first steps; imagine yourself going through the actions and envision the next steps that would naturally follow. Imagine the feelings you wish this new beginning will bring to you. With a heart full of hope, look over your left shoulder at the new moon, then with a swooping step, swing your body around to face the moon as you imagine that this is the first step upon your new journey. If you like, raise your hands to the sky as you say:

Never too early and never too late!

The moon is the key to open the gate!

I choose a new path, I choose a new fate!

New roads and new doorways, the moon will create!

• • •

May

May has a fertile and vibrant energy flow, as flowers blossom and animals come out of hiding to enjoy the sunshine and hunt for food. The Pagan holiday of Beltane is celebrated this month, traditionally marked with purification and protection rituals and fertility rites that were often centered around bonfires, wells, and wild places. This is a good month to utilize lunar energies for making wishes, increasing abundance, and casting fertility spells.

SEASONAL LUNAR SYMBOLS: Wells, white flowers, shells, water, mushrooms

COLORS: White, green, saffron yellow

ANIMALS: Bull, stag, rabbit, cow

FOLK NAMES: Flower Moon, Planting Moon, Milk Moon, Budding Moon

Full Moon Wishing Well Spell

Under the light of the full moon, make a circle of thirteen moonstones. Within this ring place four citrine stones, one each at the north, south, east, and west directions of the circle that you made with the moonstones. Think of the citrine as representing the sun, and the moonstones as representing the energies of the moon. Call on the energies of the moon to enter into the circle of stones. Imagine a wide column of lunar power streaming down from the moon and into your circle, extending deep within the earth. Use your psychic will and visualization to shape this shaft of energy into a well, envisioning an opening at the top between the rays of lunar light extending back toward the heavens. Imagine the well as a tube of space wrapped around itself, open on both ends and extending infinitely in both directions. Pull your hand in and out of this energy shaft for a moment to test the power of your magical construction. You should feel a distinct difference. If you don't, keep drawing down the lunar energy until the space extending above the circle of stones feels distinctly charged and different from the surrounding space. Once this is the case, think of your wish.

For each wish you have, hold in your hand either a small flower blossom or a silver coin, and send the essence of your wish into it. Toss the coin or flower into the "wishing well" of lunar energy you have crafted. Make as many wishes as you like, using a flower or coin to symbolize each one. Toss the items so they land within the physical ring of stones. Once you're done making your wishes, wave your hand or your wand in a circle above the ring of stones as you say:

> Moon follows earth and earth follows sun,
>
> All the wishes I have made
>
> to me will quickly come!
>
> Like moon and sun united, like land and air and sea,
>
> I won't be parted from my aim; it is a part of me!
>
> Earth sees the moon and the moon sees the sun,
>
> my wishes whispered to the moon
>
> by me will swift be won!

Leave the stones and coins or flowers in place, or wrap them together in a circle of green fabric and carry this with you until your wishes come true.

• • • SPELL 54 • • •

New Moon Spell for Fertility and Abundance

Under the waxing new moon, pour some coconut milk into a bowl and stir it clockwise as you draw down the lunar power and think of these energies blending with the sweet and fertile essences of the coconut milk, magnifying one another exponentially as their strengths are woven together. Dip your fingertips into the bowl and anoint your body with the coconut milk wherever you feel compelled to do so. You might consider putting the milk on the places of your seven major chakras, or on your pulse points. You might choose to anoint your forehead, breasts, and hands. You might decide to rub some of the milk on your lips. Just do with it whatever you feel compelled to do. Now using a silver knife or a knife with a curved blade, slice in half a pomegranate. Look at all the many seeds, and think of where you are wanting fertile energies to thrive. Are you wanting a real life, actual baby, or are you hoping instead for an artistic sort

Hecate is a lunar goddess who was worshiped in ancient Greece.

☆

chapter eight

210

of fertility that will take your expression and craftsmanship to the next level? Is it fertility in your business that you seek in hopes that profits increase and customers multiply in abundance as your company grows and thrives? Focus your thoughts on what it is you are wishing to create and as you eat some of the pomegranate seeds, imagine this manifesting just as you desire. Spread some of the remaining pomegranate seeds in a circle surrounding the bowl of coconut milk. Gaze into the bowl as you direct the remaining energy of your intention into the coconut milk. Now pour the milk over the scattered pomegranate seeds, as you envision this as a nourishing, fertile energy that will help make the things you wish for manifest and grow. Leave the bowl in the middle of the circle of seeds. In it, place a symbol of the fertility you desire. For example, you might choose a figurine of a baby if it's a child you want, or if it's fertility in your business, you might place in the bowl one of your business cards. If it's fertility for your crops, place a seed or another small part of the plants you're growing in the bowl. Leave this in place till the full moon, then take your item out of the bowl and place it on your altar or carry it with you. Fill the bowl with fresh water and drink it all, then rinse the bowl so it will be ready for its next use.

• • •

June

June is the month of the summer solstice, a time of mysticism and magic when the sun is at its apex of power—as is the moon, which reflects its light. The dividing line between the astral realm and everyday world becomes bent and blurred, creating an air of excitement and a feeling of unbounded possibility. It's a great month for magic of all sorts, but it especially favors the more fantastical realms of magic such as glamory, shapeshifting, and conjurations. It's also an excellent opportunity for divination, and to create love magic and cheering charms of all sorts.

SEASONAL LUNAR SYMBOLS: Fairies, mushrooms, quartz crystals, cup

COLORS: White, blue, silver, gold

ANIMALS: Fox, frog

FOLK NAMES: Strawberry Moon, Rose Moon, Mead Moon

• • • OTHER MAGIC 6 • • •
Full Moon Glamoury

You can use this full moon charm to create the illusion of an altered outward appearance: you might use this magic to make yourself appear more youthful or vibrant, or create a facade of smooth coolness and confidence when you're actually feeling on edge or insecure. Hold a mirror or place it so that you can see within it the reflected image of the full moon behind you. Brush your hair with a crescent-shaped comb as you envision the alterations in appearance you would like to create. Imagine that you are brushing down a cloak over yourself with each stroke of the comb, that cloak projecting the outward appearance that you are going for. If you don't have a crescent-shaped comb, you might add a lunar symbol to the handle of an ordinary brush or comb to dedicate it to the moon so that it may be used for the same purpose. Or if you prefer, you might simply invoke into your own hands the energies of the moon and then use your hands like brushes to draw over yourself a cloak of glamory. This charm fades fairly quickly, but if you do it frequently or brush your hair nightly with your special moon comb, it can have cumulative effects that linger.

• • • OTHER MAGIC 7 • • •
New Moon Divination for Guidance in Choices

Use this divination method during the waxing new moon to determine the best course of action or surest path to success when you're feeling uncertain of the way forward, or you have a decision to make and need some extra guidance. Draw a circle on a piece of paper to represent the moon. Divide the circle up like a pie, making equal sections for each potential course of action or choice you have before you. Label each section using words, symbols, or imagery to describe and depict each potential decision or choice as clearly and concisely as you can. Place the circle drawing before you on a fireproof surface that you don't mind subjecting to a bit of candle wax. Now think of the moon as you light a silver candle. Let the wax begin to melt, then drip some of it into the middle of the circle where the vertices of the pie points meet. Put the candle back in its holder and set it to the side for a minute. Now, let the wax on the paper cool for a few seconds so that it won't burn you, but get ready to take action before it completely hardens. Briefly press one of your fingertips into the spot of wax as you express your intention for guidance. Now hold the candle above the circle and with your eyes closed, tilt the candle downward so that the wax can drip off of it as you circle the candle around in thirteen complete rotations above the paper. Be sure to keep the candle well above the paper, far enough that you can confidently keep your eyes closed as the wax drips without fear of accidentally catching the paper on fire. As you drip the wax, you might chant something such as "Show me the way," or you can use this verse instead:

> Mother may I
> Ask of thee
> The best way forward
> Show to me!
> Mother may I
> May I please?
> Know the path that's best for me!
> Mother, mother,
> With the key,
> Help me find my destiny!

Put the candle back in its holder, then examine the circle you drew on the paper. The section of the pie that has the most wax on it indicates the course of action or choice that has the best potential for success. The wax may be distributed fairly evenly in two or more sections, indicating that each of these choices has potential to lead to a good outcome. Note which sections have received little or none of the wax drippings.

This indicates that conditions for this particular course of action may not be very favorable at the moment and you may face greater obstacles should you make this choice.

• • •

July

The summertime flow of good times, spontaneity, and heightened activity is at its apex in July, and we welcome our hearts to adventure. Energies are high, making this a great time of year to really press forward toward your goals and take swift action to make your dreams come true before summer comes to an end. While we want to make the most of the sunny days, the heat can sometimes be a little agitating. Sirius, the Dog Star, rises big and bright just before the sun at this time of year, an action believed by the ancient Greeks to magnify the sun's power, which could cause people to become more aggressive and hostile than usual. It's important to remember to keep your cool in July, and if you notice that tempers are starting to rise within you or around you, don't overlook the heat as a possible culprit. Try to embrace the spirit of fun that July can bring, and savor those warm summer nights when we can sit outside comfortably for as long as we like, soaking in the moonlight and dreaming of adventure. July is a good time for cheering charms, spells to boost your energy, travel magic, and spells to bring success and prosperity. As the rising heat of July can increase hostilities, it might also be a good time to renew your defenses so that you can proceed smoothly through the rest of the season with strength and confidence.

SEASONAL LUNAR SYMBOLS: Lemons, shells, magnolia, irises, orchids

COLORS: White, yellow-orange, red, blue

ANIMALS: Crab, dog, loon

FOLK NAMES: Thunder Moon, Hay Moon, Buck Moon, Crane Moon

• • • POTION 7 • • •
Full Moon Lunar Lemonade

This lunar lemonade will help to raise your spirits, boost your energy level, and encourage a whimsical spirit of fun and enchantment to surround you and embrace you. Begin by mixing up a batch of fresh lemonade using your favorite recipe. While you can substitute with ready-made store-bought lemonade, making it yourself from scratch provides you with the opportunity to infuse magic into the process every step of the way, which will help to increase the potency of the end product. If you choose not to make the lemonade yourself, just pour it from its jug into another container and spend some time stirring it. Mix the lemonade with a silver spoon if possible, letting your mind wander to thoughts of an exciting full moon night. Think of the feeling of giddiness and spontaneity that seems to fill the atmosphere as the moon glows in its fullest splendor and glory. Imagine the energy of your thoughts flowing into the lemonade, and imagine the lunar energies of the silver spoon radiating into the liquid as you stir, amplifying the lunar attributes of the lemon juice and water. Pour yourself a glass of the lemonade and place it under the light of the full moon. Take a moonstone and circle it around the outside of the glass, rubbing it on the surface of the glass at about the middle, and going all the way around its circumference in a counterclockwise direction. Make thirteen orbits with the moonstone around the glass. Now hold the lunar lemonade high toward the moon as if making a toast in honor of its magical energies and attributes you wish to imbue. Now drink deeply from the glass as you feel these lunar essences filling your being and extending throughout your energetic body and aura. When you're finished, try to do something out of the ordinary from what you usually do. Perhaps something social or artistic would fit the bill. Let the playful spirit of the moon be your chariot and let your imagination take the reins.

• • • SPELL 55 • • •
New Moon Spell for Defense

Take a nine-inch long length of black string and hold it in your hands as you think of whatever it is that you are wishing to defend yourself against. Place the string between your thumb and index finger and stroke it up and down along its entire length, then from each end toward the middle. As you handle the string, keep repeating "This is (___)," filling in the blank with the name of the person or the circumstance or whatever else it is that you are considering to be a threat. Now set the string down in front of you and clear your head for a moment. Shake off the energy from empowering the string so that you can successfully carry out the next step of the spell. It can help to rub some salt or dirt in your hands, or wash your hands with water. When you're feeling clear again and ready, make your body and aura as large as you can and imagine yourself as a giant crab, surrounded by a tough and impenetrable armor that defends you from all dangers. Imagine that you have a crab's face, able to frighten off any potential predators. Imagine that you have giant-sized pincers that you can use to snap through any obstacle, cut down any threat with one quick movement. Now pick up a pair of scissors and imagine that these scissors are your crab pincers as you cut the string representing your enemy into the tiniest possible pieces. Grind the scraps deep into the dirt or burn them completely.

• • •

August

August is an in-between sort of month. The summer has begun to wind down and we know we're steadily rolling toward fall, but we're not quite there yet. Those of us who prefer the cooler weather may be wishing that summer would hurry up and be over with already, while those of us who favor the warmth may anticipate with a sense of disappointment and dread the cooler days we know are right around the bend. The Pagan sacred day of Lughnasadh occurs in August, celebrating the first fruits of the harvest season. This month affords a good opportunity to take stock of what you have reaped from the seeds you have sown thus far, and express gratitude for the positive things in your life. It's also a good time for goal-setting and planning, and for rolling up your sleeves and heightening your resolve to get to work in making those goals a reality. magic for abundance, rituals of gratitude, and spells for strength, courage, and tenacity are all fitting themes for August lunar spellwork.

SEASONAL LUNAR SYMBOLS: Apples, cornucopia, croissant

COLORS: Golden yellow, blood red

ANIMALS: Dog, crow, owl

FOLK NAMES: Sturgeon Moon, Green Corn Moon, Blueberry Moon

• • • SPELL 56 • • •
Full Moon Spell for Further Blessings

Under an August full moon, take an apple outside and cut it in half horizontally. Hold one half of the apple in each of your hands and notice the star-like pattern of seeds within. This star can be seen as a pentacle—symbol of earth, air, fire, water, and spirit combined, the very essence of magic. Think of how this magical essence is also encapsulated by the moon, ever orbiting

The moon's diameter is 2,159 miles, a little less than the distance from New York City to Salt Lake City.

the earth and swaying its waters as it glides through space making different aspects with the fiery sun. Hold the apple halves up toward the sky and think of the energies of the stars and the moon washing over the fruit. Now hold the apple halves in front of your body as you think about all the things you are grateful for in your life. Contemplate your many blessings and let your feelings of gratitude, love, and joy toward these blessings fill your heart. Send these emotionally charged thoughts of gratitude out through your hands and into the apple halves. Kiss each half of the apple right in the middle on the little star made by the seeds as you say your thanks. Continue holding the apple halves for a few more minutes as you think of further blessings you would like to receive. Whisper your wishes into the apple, or just visualize as clearly as you can each wish coming true. Kiss the apple halves one more time and then put the halves back together, one on top of the other, and place this on the ground before you. Tap your fingertips on the top of the apple three times as you say your thanks, or use this verse to activate the spell:

> Great moon and spirits of the earth!
> On me your favors pour!
> I thank you for your many blessings!

I ask for many more!

(repeat three times)

• • • SPELL 57 • • •

New Moon Spell for Strength and Tenacity

Try this spell to give your strength and tenacity an extra boost to help you work toward your goals as you make it through summer's final push. For this spell, you'll fashion a piece of jewelry. It can be a bracelet or a necklace. You'll need a selection of stone beads that appeal to you. You'll want to find beads with large holes so that they are easy to work with. Choose beads made of stones that have lunar associations as well as attributes that increase strength or boost personal power. You might consider obsidian or onyx, quartz crystal, emerald, or jade. You might also want to include some silver beads, as well. You'll also need a special bead or pendant charm in the form of a dog. With a tenacious loyalty and willingness to serve and love unconditionally yet fight with a ferocity, the dog is the epitome of strength. Their associations with the underworld and with the nighttime make them a fitting lunar symbol. Place all your beads in front of you with the dog bead in the middle. Now touch your fingertips to the dog bead or hold it in your hand and visualize for a moment. Imagine a large and powerful dog standing on a hill in front of you, a waxing crescent moon behind it. Imagine that though the dog looks tremendously strong, you are not at all afraid because you know this dog is your friend and a loyal, fierce protector. Imagine that this powerful dog looks at you, then excitedly bounds toward you as if to greet you. Imagine that you open your arms wide to welcome the dog and that it leaps not only into your arms, but into your soul, its spirit entering into your spirit, imparting to you its own strength and tenacious power and endurance. Now touch or hold each of the other beads in turn, thinking of the energies of these beads magnifying and becoming even stronger. Think of the strength of stone, its hardness, its impenetrability. Think of the magical qualities of each stone resonating and harmonizing with your own desires for greater strength and tenacity. When you're finished empowering the beads, braid together a white, black, and red string and arrange the beads upon this to form your jewelry. If you prefer, you can use a single string in white, gold, or silver. You may want to create your jewelry over the course of several nights, adding more beads as the moon waxes. When you've finished arranging the beads, tie off the bracelet or necklace with nine knots and wear to boost your strength, tenacity, and power.

• • •

September

September is the month of the autumn equinox, ushering another harvest as the earth transitions and transforms. Temperatures are getting cooler, and we begin to gather indoors more often, enjoying friendships and taking pleasure in the resulting fruits of our labor. This is a good time to give thanks for our continuing blessings and abundance, and to celebrate and nourish our relationships with those with love.

SEASONAL LUNAR SYMBOLS: Mooncakes, cornucopia, apple, scythe, wine, mushrooms

COLORS: Golden yellow, white

ANIMALS: Fox, stag, hawk, blackbird, owl, eagle, toad

FOLK NAMES: Harvest Moon, Corn Moon, Barley Moon

• • • SPELL 58 • • •
Full Moon Spell for Togetherness

Use this spell to celebrate and increase feelings of togetherness shared with family and friends. If you're able to do so, invite some of your loved ones to share in this magic with you. If you're not able to have anyone with you there

The moon has an iron core and a partially molten mantle believed to be comprised of minerals such as olivine and pyroxene. The crust of the moon is composed primarily of anorthosite and basalt.

physically, imagine them with you in spirit. Under a full moon in September, spread out a blanket or set up a table outside. On the table, place an assortment of celebratory foods. You might choose moon cakes or lemon cookies, grapes, breads, fruits, wine, or other foods. Also arrange on the table an assortment of photographs or place cards to represent not only your ancestors but your living relatives and friends as well. Look to the moon and think of your feelings of love and gratitude toward your friends and family. Think of how the moon links us all, and how we all depend on it. Clasp hands with your loved ones around the spread of food and envision the moonlight flowing through your bodies, from hand to hand, linking everyone present with an invisible thread of lunar light and power. If you're doing the ritual alone, spread your arms wide as if you are embracing the spirits of your dear ones in a loving hug. Say this verse if you like, or simply spend some time enjoying the feeling of love and letting this energy magnify and strengthen your bonds:

Bound by our hearts!

Bound by love!

Bound by the light of the moon up above!

Together we live!

Together we love!

Together we're bound by the moon up above!

Enjoy the food and spend time indulging in pleasant memories and divulging your hopes and dreams for the future.

• • • SPELL 59 • • •
New Moon Spell for Abundance

At the first appearance of the waxing new moon, begin this spell. Begin by procuring or making a cornucopia. If you can't find one in a store, you can make one out of vines, bake one out of dough, or even fashion one with sturdy paper and tape as a last resort. If you prefer, you might use a crescent-shaped basket instead. Take the cornucopia outside and hold it aloft toward the sky. Notice how the shape of the cornucopia mimics the shape of the waxing crescent moon. Think of the cultivated crops and wild plants growing abundantly in the moonlight. Think of the things in your own life that you wish to grow in abundance. Now act as if you are scooping up the moonlight as well as your wishes into the cornucopia, moving it through the air as if it is a large scoop or a cup. Say to yourself, "I have it now!" Then place the cornucopia on your altar, filling it with items to symbolize your wishes. You might choose an apple to symbolize abundant health, flowers to symbolize abundant love, or coins to symbolize abundant wealth. You might choose stones, plants, or even drawings to represent the abundance you desire. Add another item to the cornucopia each day until the moon or the cornucopia is full—whichever comes first. Then share, repurpose, give away, or give back to the earth all the items you have placed inside the cornucopia. The spell will quickly bring abundance.

• • •

October

Leaves curl up and fall off the trees as the final harvest of the growing season is gathered and we all prepare for the colder, darker days ahead. October plunges nature into survival mode, as many plants die or go dormant, and fewer animals and birds can be seen moving about as the changing weather calls many species to hunker down and hibernate, or migrate to warmer locales. In Celtic lands, the sacred day of Samhain was celebrated in October, a time that marked the start of a new year and spirits of the dead were believed to roam, paying visits to their loved ones as well as to their enemies. Many witches and Pagans today make special effort to honor the spirits of the dead throughout the month of October. It's an excellent time for moon magic intended to aid in conjuring spirits, communicating with the dead, and letting go of that which is past. It's a time of year to embrace the inevitable transformation that the coming winter will bring. What is spent and done must be shed away, but this sacrifice of letting go will enable new perspective and growth to come.

SEASONAL LUNAR SYMBOLS: Cauldron, scythe, key, mushrooms

COLORS: Black, gray, purple, golden orange

ANIMALS: Rat, owl, bat, cat, dog, spider, coyote

FOLK NAMES: Hunter's Moon, Blood Moon, Dying Grass Moon

• • • SPELL 60 • • •
Full Moon Spell to Call on the Dead

Use this magic to help guide spirits of the dead to wander your way for a visit. Procure a large turnip, cut off the top, and hollow it out as if you were carving a pumpkin.

Slice off a small bit of the bottom of the turnip so that it will sit flat without tilting over. Use a pumpkin-carving tool to carve a pleasant and welcoming face in the flesh of the turnip. Put a small tealight candle inside the turnip, and place it on a fireproof dish near your front door. As you light the candle flame, think of the full moon and its glorious illumination. Think of the flame glowing within the turnip as being connected to the full moon, and think of the full moon as being a large, round open door or window of sorts, a portal between the worlds of the living and the dead. On a small scrap of paper, write the name of the spirit with which you wish to visit. Think of your desire to feel their presence and let this desire flow into the name you have written. Hold the paper with a set of tongs and burn it in the candle flame. As the paper burns, speak the person's name and focus on your desire to visit with them. Let the ashes fall inside the turnip. Leave the candle burning within the turnip, keeping it on the fireproof dish just in case. You can then utilize tools of spirit communication, or simply proceed with your night with an especially watchful eye for any signs of visitors not in the flesh. Be sure to keep a pleasant atmosphere after inviting the dead to visit you. You want to be a good and pleasant host just as you would for any other guest.

• • • SPELL 61 • • •

Dark Moon Spell to Bring Forth Spirits

Use this spell during the dark moon to aid in summoning spirits of the dead. Once the spirits are present, you might use a talking board, automatic writing, a pendulum, tarot cards, channeling, or other means of spirit communication, or you might simply choose to honor the spirits with an offering and express your feelings toward their memory. To begin the spell, place some mugwort in a cauldron filled with water and heat it up until steam begins to rise off the water. Pour a glass of wine (or grape juice) and place it on one side of the cauldron, saying as you do so that the wine is for your intended guest. Speak their name and imagine that you are setting out the wine for them to come and drink. On the other side of the cauldron, place a key, preferably an old skeleton key. If you like and you don't have any allergies or breathing issues, inhale some of the vapor of the mugwort brew as you clear your mind of all else but thoughts of the soul with whom you wish to commune. Breathe deeply and slowly. Imagine the spirit you seek emerging from the moon as you begin to rotate the key in a counterclockwise direction, making a total of nine complete rotations. As you turn the key, say this verse, spinning the key in three complete rotations with each stanza, and increasing the speed for the last set of rotations that accompany the final stanza, which should be recited with greatest emphasis:

Dark mother!

Hecate!

You who holds the key!

Please send forth (name of the spirit)!

Keeper of the cauldron!

Guardian of the gateway!

I call on you to

please send forth (name of the spirit)!

Turn the key!

Open the gate!

Hecate!

Send forth (name of the spirit)!

Sit still in silence for a few moments and open your senses to any spirits present. If it doesn't seem that your invited guest is going to show, you might try again with a different name. When it seems that you can sense a presence, proceed with your planned spirit communication activities, or simply sit quietly and see what feelings and impressions come to you. When you're finished, express your thanks to the spirits, then tell them to depart. You might say something like, "By the moon's bright blessings, I bid you farewell."

• • •

November

The colder, darker days of November turn our attentions inward toward our hearts and homes as shelter becomes a need and warmth becomes a rare commodity. This month lends itself to both solitary introspection, and experiences of togetherness with those we love. Many Americans celebrate the Thanksgiving holiday in November, marking yet another harvest-themed celebration. This month also continues the theme of honoring the dead. As the trees are bare and the ground cold and barren, we come face to face with death in Nature. We can find peace in this stillness. November invites us to contemplate the mystery of life, death, and rebirth as we witness this cycle occur in the world around us. The flow of energy this month invites us to meditation and introspection, to divination and psychic intuition. This is a good time for moon magic to heal the living or help the dead, as well as for protective spellwork to strengthen your defenses as you make ready to plunge into winter.

SEASONAL LUNAR SYMBOLS: Cornucopia, mushrooms, black scrying mirror, round black stones

COLORS: Black, gray, golden orange

ANIMALS: Scorpion, goose, wolf, racoon, beaver

FOLK NAMES: Beaver Moon, Frost Moon, Mourning Moon

• • • SPELL 62 • • •
Full Moon Spell for Blessing Graves

Use this spell to help soothe the souls of the dead by means of purifying and blessing neglected graves. On a full moon, take a sprig of juniper or rosemary and a cup of spring water to the grave you wish to tend to. First, sit next to the grave and focus on the soul who once occupied the body that lies within it. Try to tune in with the spirit and see if you can sense anything or if you receive any messages. Now think of your desire to bring this spirit peace and comfort. Look up to the moon and focus on your desire for assistance in bringing healing and comfort to the dead. Feel the moonlight flowing down on the grave, cleansing it and washing away from that spirit any lingering sorrow, anger, or regret. Now utilize your own powers, moving your hand slowly above the grave and gravestone as you imagine that you are drawing off any negative energies. Cast these energies to the side, shaking your hand and making a motion as if tossing something away from your body and into the ground. Take care that the energy does not get thrown into another gravesite, and try to neutralize the energy as much as you can before casting it aside. To do so, imagine that moonlight is filling your hand, transporting that unwanted energy to the moon where it will be neutralized and transformed into something new. Once you feel you have cleared as much of the negative energy from the gravesite as possible, fill your heart with a feeling of love and caring. Think of the moon's soft, silvery light as you brush the juniper or rosemary gently over the grave and gravestone, envisioning a loving, healing, soothing energy rushing out of the leaves and into the grave to soothe the wandering soul of the being whose shell still lays there. Remove any weeds or debris from the gravesite. Finally, hold the cup of water up to the moon and open yourself to assistance in the work at hand. Envision the energies of the moon filling the cup, transforming it into a healing elixir that will bring peace to the dead. Pour this cup of water slowly over the top of the gravestone as you say:

Isis is an Egyptian goddess associated with the moon and fertility.

Child of the moon,
you are remembered!
May you rest in peace
till the wheel turns anew!

Kiss your fingertips and touch them to the gravestone, then place the sprig of juniper or rosemary on the grave and leave it there. Walk away abruptly and swiftly without looking back. Rub your hands together, shake them, and touch the earth or a tree to help break the connection to the spirit as you leave the area.

New Moon Spell to Overcome Enemies

Use this spell as an additional line of support to help get rid of harmful individuals. If someone is harming you or threatening to harm you or your loved ones, please report it right away to law enforcement, tell the people in your life what's going on, and keep your doors locked—*then* do some magic. Take care of the more obvious and easy to carry out means of defense first before you worry about doing any spellwork. This magic can also be used to help weaken and break down the harmful constructs in the world that cause suffering to many. Cast this spell on a dark moon or young new moon. You'll need a small scrap of paper and a pen, a small black pouch, a bent nail made of iron, and some sort of image of a scorpion. This can be a small drawing, a figurine, a piece of jewelry, or anything else that depicts the image of a scorpion. Hold this scorpion emblem in your hands and imagine in your mind that it is a real-life scorpion, only it is friendly to you. Cradle it lovingly in your hands as if it were your pet or familiar. Think of the moon, ever watchful over the earth even when it's obscured from our view or when we cannot see but the thinnest sliver of its glow. Think of your scorpion as also having this same ever-watchful quality, moving invisibly in the shadows until it spots its prey, then quickly coming out to strike in a burst of fierce power. Focus on the scorpion's curved stinger, and see in your mind's eye superimposed on this stinger the crescent moon. Visualize the lunar energy fusing itself within the scorpion's stinger, causing it to glow with a bright white light. See in your mind's eye this power radiating from the scorpion, and envision this power being so strong that it pushes away any potential danger. Now write down the name of your enemy, be it a particular individual, or an evil that affects all of society, such as the evil of sexual assault or hate crimes. If it's a specific individual who is your enemy, reserve this spell for only the most extreme of cases. The results can be rather harsh if the person is indeed a threat to you; if they're not actually a serious threat, the backlash from your working could be severe. Place the name of your foe in the pouch along with the scorpion symbol and the nail, piercing the nail through the scrap of paper. Tie the pouch closed tightly using nine knots. As you tie the knots, say these words to help lock in the magic:

Scorpion, powerful being of night!

Friend of the moon with its piercing light!

I ask you here to fight this fight!

This is your enemy to smite, smite, smite!

Your scorpion's sting like the moon's silver scythe!

You strike down my enemies

cold in the night!

Like the moon's silver blade,

like the moon's silver light,

all fall to your sting in the darkness of night!

With the moon's growing light,

with the moon's growing blade,

your sting will grow stronger!

The price will be paid!

Keep this pouch somewhere hidden and secret until the threat has passed, or until the next dark moon—whichever is soonest, then dispose of it somewhere away from your home where you don't usually frequent.

• • •

December

December brings us the winter solstice, the tilting point that brings us back to the point where the days will begin to get a little bit longer, although the night is still in the lead. Yule and other holiday festivities dominate the month, bringing friends and family together to give gifts and make pleasant memories that add to the tapestry of our personal traditions and celebrations. December offers an atmosphere of joy, love, and hope that can add extra fuel to your moon magic. Spells for abundance and success, spells to increase joy, and spells to encourage togetherness, compassion, and cooperation are all great choices for December moon magic.

SEASONAL LUNAR SYMBOLS: Holly, brazil nuts, ice, snow

COLORS: Green, red, white, silver

ANIMALS: Reindeer, stag, goat, moon bear

FOLK NAMES: Cold Moon, Oak Moon, Long Nights Moon

Full Moon Spell for Bestowing and Receiving Gifts

Use this spell to help bring blessings upon yourself and your loved ones. Ideally, share the spell with those you love. If this isn't possible, you can simply visualize the people that you wish could be with you, or you might create name cards or use dolls or stuffed animals to stand in their place. Fill a bowl with brazil nuts, and place it outside for a few minutes under a December full moon. Notice how the shape of the nuts resembles the moon in its waxing phase. Swirl the nuts around as you invite the power of the full moon to enter into them. Bring the nuts back inside so that you can be warmer and more comfortable for the rest of the spell. Place the bowl in the middle of a comfortable area, and have everyone who is taking part in the spell gather closely around it. Take turns, or act spontaneously as each individual feels compelled, taking a nut from the bowl and presenting it to one of the others as if it is a gift. As you hand each other the nuts, name each one as something else, a bigger blessing that you wish to bestow upon the person. For instance, you might say "I give you abundance!" as you hand a nut to your Uncle Henry, or you could utter "I give you great happiness!" as you give a nut to your friend Eleanor. Encourage everyone present to give the nuts freely to each other, saying whatever positive thing comes to mind that they wish for the person as they give each nut. If you're doing this spell alone, simply place the nuts into separate piles as you think of each person and the gifts you wish for them to receive. Be sure to give yourself some nuts as well, and if you're doing this spell with others present, be sure to encourage them to do the same. As you take nuts for yourself from the bowl, you might say something like, "I receive the gift of greater success in all my endeavors," or whatever else it is specifically that you are wishing for. After the nuts have all been divvied up, eat them or share them at a food bank. If it's okay to do so where you live, you might leave just a few of the nuts outside as a special treat for the squirrels or birds to enjoy.

• • • SPELL 65 • • •
New Moon Spell for Manifesting Resources

During a waxing new moon, draw a set of antlers on a piece of paper, emphasizing the crescent-like curve. Lay this flat on your altar, and on the paper, place a moonstone in the middle of the open space between the antlers you have drawn. Now think of the resources you need to manifest and draw a symbol for each resource on either side of the moonstone between the antlers. Now think of the lunar energies drawing to you what you need, and imagine a stag bringing to you on its antlers the resources you desire. Surround the image with boughs of holly and envision the nourishing, protective energies of the holly flowing toward your drawing and the magical intentions it represents. Now move the moonstone back and forth between the antlers, gliding it over the symbols you have drawn. Return the moonstone back to its original place in the center of the antlers and leave this in place with the holly boughs to help quickly manifest the resources you request.

• • •

Making Your Own Lunar Traditions

You can deepen your practice of moon magic further by creating your own rituals, spells, and traditions to celebrate the moon throughout the year. What you do doesn't have to be fancy, or complicated, or anything that has come from a book. It should, however, come from the heart! Honor who you are and design magical rituals and traditions that speak to you. If you love to cook, you might want to create some lunar magic traditions that center around a special recipe. If you like to make jewelry, you might create a new design to mark a special lunar occasion such as a full moon or an eclipse. Celebrating the moon regularly and often in ways that are personally meaningful to us is the key to feeling truly connected to the moon and its magic.

CONCLUSION

You've learned a vast variety of moon spells in this book, but that doesn't mean there aren't infinite other possibilities for your moon magic. Explore, try new things, practice, and follow your intuition, and you'll continuously discover more about your own ways to attune to the moon. You'll also get increasingly better at working with its energies. Indeed, through regular practice, you'll find that you have your own utterly unique ways of making moon magic, being the utterly unique creature that you are. The moon is a powerful force of nature, and so too are you.

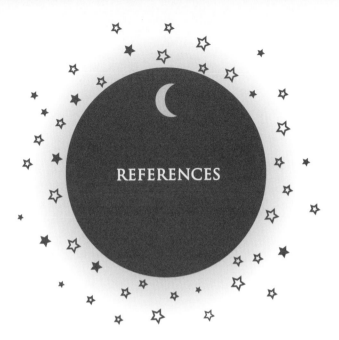

REFERENCES

Agrippa, Henry Cornelius. *The Philosophy of Natural Magic.* Chicago: de Laurence, Scott and Company, 1913, via sacred-texts.com: https://www.sacred-texts.com/eso/pnm/index.htm#contents.

Conway, D. J. *Moon Magic.* St. Paul, MN: Llewellyn Publications, 1995.

Cunningham, Scott. *The Complete Book of Incense, Oils, and Brews.* St. Paul, MN: Llewellyn Publications, 1989.

George, Llewellyn. *The New A to Z Horoscope Maker and Delineator.* 1910. Rev. ed. St. Paul, MN: Llewellyn Publications, 1985.

Vernon, Joy. "The Moon Through the Signs" Joy Vernon.com: https://joyvernon.com/blog/the-moon-through-the-signs/.

RESOURCES

ThePlanetsToday.com
Nasa.gov/moon
Moon3dMap.com
TimeandDate.com/moon/phases/